CASTLES

OF BRITAIN AND IRELAND

CASTLES

OF BRITAIN AND IRELAND

RODNEY
CASTLEDEN

METRO BOOKS
New York

CONTENTS

The numbers preceding the names are the key
to the site locations shown on the map opposite.

SCOTLAND

IRELAND

ENGLAND

WALES

INTRODUCTION

Today we see castles as picturesque relics of a romantic past, as left-overs from the chivalry of the middle ages. But when they were built they were seen as symbols of raw power, both by the kings and barons who built them and by the ordinary people they were meant to intimidate. Castles were largely associated with oppression and extortion; they were expensive to build and maintain and the cost nearly always fell upon the common people.

These buildings speak of different levels of struggle for supremacy. Some were built by knights or lords to show their social superiority over the common people around them. Some were built by barons engaging in wars with one another, for status and territory. Some were built by kings struggling to weld a nation by limiting the power of insubordinate barons or to exert supremacy over other nations.

A parallel can be drawn with the abbeys and cathedrals built during this period. Though their purpose was ostensibly for the worship of God, the rich and sumptuous architecture of these buildings was also designed to demonstrate the power wielded by the church.

Although we think of castles in terms of the stone structures we see today, their ancestry stretches back to a more distant past. As early as 1000 BC, there were enclosures that were unmistakably created for military

defence. These late Bronze Age hillforts and their Iron Age successors were often laid out on hill tops and they were apparently intended to function as refuges for whole communities. Similar earthwork enclosures, often with timber palisades along the banks, were built in the Dark Ages after the Romans left Britain. These too were serious defensive works and major community projects. The Romans, however, built in stone and they raised impressive structures that really were castles – remodellings in stone of temporary military camps. Later, the Saxons probably built timber castles; these were fortified palaces defended by stout palisades, watchtowers and ditches – the bare ingredients of a medieval castle.

With the Norman invasion came the greatest period of castle-building, and for 500 years powerful lords exerted and flaunted their influence through the strength and magnificence of their castles, which became mighty symbols of power. In England this era came to an end quite suddenly, when the Civil War showed conclusively that the masonry simply could not stand up to evolving weapons technology. Many were slighted – deliberately disabled to put them out of commission – by Oliver Cromwell.

The great age of castles coincided closely with the great age of cathedrals and abbeys. They too were huge, complex and expensive structures built of stone, designed to impress. Although ecclesiastical buildings, many of these came under attack from invaders and some became places of refuge, so these too had to be sturdily built. In England, it was not the Civil War that brought about their fall but the greed of Henry VIII a hundred years earlier. Even so, the slighting had the same effect, of creating picturesque ruins that have become irresistibly romantic symbols of a bygone age. More than that, however, they are some of the most important visible relics of Britain's history.

It's clear that castles and abbeys represent a major link to the complex events of the past and are powerful touchstones to the imagination. The stories of these great buildings give their own distinct perspectives on history, whether it concerns border skirmishes, the Spanish Armada, the fall of a monarch, or the Jacobite rebellions.

Today, some surviving castles have become mansions, still functioning as family homes, while the role of most abbeys and cathedrals has reverted to its original, purer purpose. Many others are tourist attractions or museums. Only a selection can be included here, but the intention is to offer a taste of the great diversity of fortified buildings that provide such tangible reminders of a turbulent past.

SCOTLAND

DUNROBIN CASTLE

LOCATION **HIGHLAND, SCOTLAND**

DATE BUILT **1834–48**

FOUNDER **DUKE OF SUTHERLAND**

Dunrobin Castle is a cross between a French chateau and a fairytale palace – or a creation of Walt Disney – and altogether the unlikeliest building to stumble upon in the Scottish Highlands. It stands north of Dornoch Firth on the edge of a sea-cliff amongst green and luxuriant grounds.

Dunrobin is a fascinating place, not quite real, a sort of secret garden in the Highlands. In spite of having the impeccably well-groomed appearance of a great mansion, it is in fact a real castle and a very ancient one. The Scottish kings who took Sutherland back from the Norsemen in the 12th century granted it to Hugh de Moravia; Hugh's son William was created Earl of Sutherland in 1235. Dunrobin is mentioned in documents as being the stronghold of the Earls of Sutherland in 1401, but the ancient tower that survives, all but hidden, at the very heart of the building may well be older than that.

The Earldom of Sutherland is the oldest in Scotland and by ancient tradition if there are no male heirs the earldom may pass through the female line. When this actually happened in the 16th century it led to a fierce and bloody dispute. When it happened again in the 17th century the result was more peaceable but it still led to a long and costly legal dispute. The Sutherland estate is a very substantial piece of property indeed – and one that is well worth fighting for. The law eventually decided in favour of Elizabeth, whose father, the 18th earl, had died when she was one year old. She became 19th countess and married an Englishman, George Leveson-Gower, who was shortly afterwards to become Marquess of Stafford; shortly before his death he was created Duke of Sutherland. This is a rare example of a man enhancing his social status by marriage – but then everything about Dunrobin is rare and out of the ordinary.

The marriage of Elizabeth and George led to the creation of one of the wealthiest and most brilliant families in 19th-century Britain. When her husband was English ambassador to France, the 'countess-duchess'

The formal gardens were laid out in 1850 by
Sir Charles Barry, the architect who built
the Victorian extension to Dunrobin and also
the Houses of Parliament in London.

lent her clothes to Marie-Antoinette for the desperate escape attempt that she and her family made; they were stopped, recognized and arrested at Varennes. The first duke inherited the duke of Bridgewater's fortune in addition to his own; he was described as a 'Leviathan of Wealth'. An enormous statue of him stands on a mountainside near Golspie. But he was a callous landowner, lacking in common humanity. To make himself even richer, he was responsible for ordering the Highland Clearances. Many crofters were forcibly and cruelly turned off their land. While some like to blame the factors and other employees who carried out the duke's orders to evict, the duke must be held responsible for giving the orders. One of his successors, the third Duke of Sutherland, who by then owned 1.3 million acres, was to become the biggest landowner in Western Europe.

Most of the exterior of the castle was built by the second duke, who commissioned Sir Charles Barry to design additions to the 18th-century house in French Renaissance style, complete with picturesque dormer windows and high pointed conical tower roofs. Work began in 1834 to Barry's design, with slight modifications by the building contractor, W. Leslie of Aberdeen. Barry visited Dunrobin in 1848, and designed the imposing entrance tower.

Caen stone, imported all the way from France, was used for the staircase. This is architecturally the finest part of the castle's interior; much of Dunrobin was gutted when fire broke out in 1915 while the castle was being used as a naval hospital. When the First World War was over, the burnt-out rooms were redesigned by Sir Robert Lorimer, and repaired and redecorated. Lorimer created a panelled dining room, where five big family portraits hang. There is a painting of the second duchess, Harriet, by Franz Zaver Winterhalter; she was Mistress of the Robes and a close friend of Queen Victoria, who stayed at Dunrobin Castle more than once.

Lorimer created the long drawing room out of two earlier rooms. Here two magnificent paintings by Canaletto are on display, along with some fine French furniture. There is a vaulted corridor, from which there is a view of the castle's ancient tower and courtyard.

In the gardens below the terraces there is a castle museum. This was once a banqueting house, but during the course of the 19th century it filled up with a collection of curiosities, including 400 animal heads, as well as other oddments such as weapons, coins, Lord Raglan's cap, Garibaldi's slippers and Queen Victoria's handkerchief. The collection also includes the skulls of the sons of King Lochlin of Denmark. It is not a museum in any modern sense, but a fine example of an 18th- or 19th-century 'cabinet of curiosities' and therefore a museum piece in itself.

Dunrobin Castle is a delightful creation and the family that created it is full of interest, but it is an extremely uncomfortable thought for many of us that this huge display of wealth was built on the misery of the first Duke of Sutherland's tenants; already extremely poor, many of them were dispossessed, and often brutally, in the interests of further profit for their callous landlord.

EILEAN DONAN CASTLE

LOCATION **HIGHLAND, SCOTLAND**

DATE BUILT **13TH CENTURY**

Eilean Donan is the ultimate picturesque Highland castle, perched on a little rocky island in a loch. It has its roots deeply implanted in remote antiquity. The name itself means 'Island of Donan', referring to a hermit who lived there in the seventh century.

Opposite the castle is a human footprint carved in the living rock. This tells us that the place was a royal centre in the Dark Ages and possibly much earlier still. There is a similar footprint at Tintagel in Cornwall, which was probably used for oath-taking ceremonies such as coronations.

The hermit Donan moved to a monastic foundation on the island of Eigg, where in 618 he was set upon by marauders and beheaded along with 52 of his companions.

The castle that we now see dates from the late 13th century. Only archaeological investigation can now determine whether the remains of Viking-period defences lie underneath the stone keep and its outer enclosing wall. In 1263 a vast Viking fleet made its way south along the west coast of Scotland, past Eilean Donan, to engage Alexander III of Scotland at Largs. The invaders were resoundingly defeated and limped back to Norway. This event marked the end of 400 years of Scandinavian control. By the Treaty of Perth of 1266, the Highlands and Islands passed to the Scottish Crown.

By the end of the 13th century Eilean Donan had passed into the hands of KennethMackenzie, in spite of repeated attempts by the Earl of Ross to take it from him.

Tradition has it that John Mackenzie sheltered Robert the Bruce at Eliean Donan when he was out of favour with many of the clan chiefs and being hunted by the English. By 1331, Robert's fortunes had changed; he had defeated his enemies and established himself as King of Scotland.

The dispute over the ownership of the castle between the Mackenzies and the Earls of Ross continued. The Earl threatened to take it by force, but a royal charter of 1362 (from King David II) confirmed the Mackenzies' title, and they managed to hold the castle for the next two centuries. The MacRaes had settled in the district and they became known as the Mackenzies' 'Coat of Mail', their bodyguard. But the Earldom of Ross had not given up. When Euphemia Countess of Ross was widowed for the second time in 1427, she cast about for a third husband, and her eye fell on the young Alexander Mackenzie (and his castle). He turned her down and she promptly had him thrown in prison. The Constable of Eilean Donan retaliated by taking one of her kinsmen as a hostage to exchange for the young Mackenzie. The Countess agreed the exchange and Alexander Mackenzie was released.

In the late 15th century the castle shrank. The old enclosure wall was dismantled and new defences were raised enclosing a smaller precinct. The MacRaes became constables of the castle in 1509 and took control of the whole district. The Lordship of the Isles had been extinguished as a political force, but in 1530 Donald Gorm MacDonald of Sleat foolishly tried to revive it for himself. Nine years later, Donald sailed to Applecross with 50 galleys to lay waste the Mackenzie lands before heading for Eilean Donan, which was rumoured to be lightly garrisoned.

The castle was indeed lightly garrisoned: it was held by only three men, the constable John Matheson, the young Duncan MacRae and a watchman. They bravely shut the gate against Donald's soldiers, who resorted to firing arrows at the windows. One of these hit Matheson, leaving only the watchman and Duncan McRae. They ran short of ammunition. Duncan was left with only one barbed arrow, which he kept by him until he could use it to good effect. Donald used a battering ram to force the gate; then Duncan shot him in the foot. Donald impatiently pulled the arrow out and in doing so severed one of his own arteries. The bleeding was so intense that the MacDonalds withdrew in haste, putting the injured Donald MacDonald into a boat and landing him near Avernish at a place called Larachtaigh Mhic-Dhomhnuill, 'the site of MacDonald's house'. There he bled to death. It was an historic moment, marking the end of the Lordship of the Isles.

Gunpowder changed everything. It may be that the hornwork added to the south-east angle of the castle in the 15th century was created to accommodate new guns.

Three years after the failure of the 1715 Stuart rebellion, a plot was hatched to try to land a large force of Spaniards in England and a smaller force of Spaniards and Jacobites in Scotland, and there meet the Highland contingent. The 'armada' sailing to England was badly crippled but the smaller contingent reached Scotland, landing close to Eilean Donan. A force under General Wightman set out from Inverness to intercept the Jacobite force. In May 1719 three naval vessels under Captain Boyle sailed into Kintail and laid siege to Eilean Donan, capturing it after a short bombardment. Troops from the ships entered the castle and used its own ammunition stores to blow it up, at least to the extent of rendering it unusable.

Another version of events is also told, which has the defenders of the castle, Colonel Donald Murchison and Christopher MacRae, deliberately sabotaging the castle to prevent it from falling into Government hands.

The ruins were neglected for 200 years until 1912, when Lt.-Col. John MacRae-Gilstrap bought it and began restoration work. He was helped by Farquhar MacRae who had had a dream telling him exactly what the original structure had looked like; this was later confirmed by plans held in Edinburgh Castle. The beautifully rebuilt castle was finished in 1932, together with a bridge to the mainland, and is now open to the public. The kitchen and bedrooms can be seen, as well as the barrel-vaulted Billeting Room for off-duty soldiers. There is a very fine Banqueting Hall in romantic baronial style, containing a display of Jacobite memorabilia – including a lock of Bonnie Prince Charlie's hair.

FYVIE CASTLE

LOCATION **ABERDEENSHIRE, SCOTLAND**

DATE BUILT **13TH CENTURY**

Fyvie Castle is the finest example there is of Scottish baronial architecture. It bears witness to the various stages of its development, each addition representing the tastes and preoccupations of a generation.

The castle has five towers, each one built by and named after one of the five families who owned Fyvie in succession. On the south side, the Meldrum Tower stands on the left, the Preston Tower on the right. In the centre the Seton Tower forms a grand arched entrance; this tall, spectacular and highly original gatehouse was the work of Alexander Seton, the Earl of Dunfermline, in 1599. The Gordon Tower was added in 1777 and the Leith Tower was built in 1899. This may sound like a hotch-potch of add-ons and extensions, but the overall effect is extremely harmonious.

The castle is three lofty storeys high but mostly only one room deep, with the rooms opening into one another. The great set-piece of the castle interior is the elaborate processional staircase, which was built by Seton in 1605. Strongly influenced by contemporary French architecture, it is lavishly decorated with heraldry.

The first significant documented record of Fyvie is in 1296, when Edward I visited. A little later, the castle became one of Robert the Bruce's royal residences; he set aside a tract of the adjoining countryside as a royal hunting forest. In 1397 Fyvie Castle passed into the hands of the Preston family; it was Sir Henry Preston, who fought at the Battle of Otterburn, who built one of the towers. In 1596, Fyvie was bought from the Meldrums by Alexander Seton, another of the tower-builders. Seton achieved a peerage, and attended Parliament as the first Lord Fyvie.

The castles and its estate were seized by the Crown in 1689, following the death of the third Lord Fyvie; he made the mistake of fighting on the wrong side at the Battle of Killiecrankie. In the 1740s, Fyvie passed into the hands of the Gordons. This was the family that produced Lord Byron, and the traditional dance, the Gay Gordons.

CRAIGIEVAR CASTLE

LOCATION **ABERDEENSHIRE, SCOTLAND**

DATE BUILT **1626**

FOUNDER **WILLIAM FORBES**

Craigievar is like a castle out of a fairytale, taller than it is wide, with soaring walls and a roofline that bristles with gables, chimneys, corbelled round corner turrets and conical spires.

Craigievar's setting too is straight out of a fairytale. It stands just to the south of the village of Muir of Fowlis near Alford in a beautifully landscaped park, surrounded by trees, shrubs and sloping lawns.

The reality is that Craigievar Castle is of no great antiquity. It was built in 1626 by William Forbes as a tower house. Forbes was a merchant from Aberdeen, who had made a fortune trading with ports in the Baltic. Like many another Scottish tower house it was built on an L-shaped ground plan and rises to six storeys high. Built to standard Scottish fortress specifications, it had only a few small windows in the lower walls, heavy doors and an iron yett (a gate in the form of a heavy grille). It also had a surrounding curtain wall with a squat round tower at each corner, though only one has survived.

In spite of these expensive design features, Craigievar Castle was to serve primarily as a stately home rather than as a real fortress. In fact, by the time it was built in the 1620s, the age of the castle-fortress was over. Weapons technology had developed to a point where masonry could not withstand an attack by cannon. The tower house nevertheless continued to be a good defence against casual raiders. Perhaps more important, castle architecture had become associated with status, so high-status families still wanted castles.

Craigievar Castle's interior was luxuriously appointed and much has survived unchanged from the 17th century. There are some fine Jacobean vaulted and plastered ceilings and Jacobean panelling to match. Its period charm made it an early attraction for tourists, and its reputation was greatly enhanced by a visit from Queen Victoria and Prince Albert.

This castle was never abandoned, but remained in occupation by its owners, William Forbes and his descendants, for most of its history. It was only in 1963 that it passed into the hands of the National Trust for Scotland.

SLAINS CASTLE

LOCATION **ABERDEENSHIRE, SCOTLAND**

DATE BUILT **16TH CENTURY**

FOUNDER **HAY FAMILY**

The broken shell of Old Slains Castle stands on the windswept sea-cliffs between Aberdeen and Peterhead. This was a seat of the Hay family, the Earls of Erroll.

The lands belonging to Slains were given to Sir Gilbert Hay by Robert the Bruce as a reward for his services in the armed struggle against the English. Sir Gilbert was also appointed High Constable of Scotland.

Sir Gilbert was succeeded by his son Sir David, who went with David II to the Battle of Neville's Cross in 1346; the king was captured and Sir David was killed. William Hay was created Earl of Erroll and Lord of Slains by James II as a reward for his support in the king's war against the 'Black' Douglas lords and their allies, the Lyndsays and the MacDonalds. The rebel lords were eventually defeated by the Gordons and the 'Red' Douglas. The Hays were allies of the Gordons.

The tower of Old Slains dates from around this time. It was an oblong keep five storeys high, with a vaulted basement entered at courtyard level. The second storey was entered, English-style, by an external staircase, in this case a collapsible wooden staircase, a little like some old iron fire escapes. The battlements were probably fitted with bartizans, or open, roofless turrets, at each corner. There was a pitched roof with chimneys on top. There was also an overhanging box machicolation positioned directly above the staircase entrance. This was installed not just to bomb attackers trying to force open the door, but to ensure the destruction of the staircase itself in time of siege. Inside the tower there was a stone spiral staircase that connected all the different levels from the second storey upwards.

To begin with, in the 15th century, the tower was surrounded by a wooden palisade. Beyond that it was protected on three sides by the cliffs and on the fourth side by a ditch. In the early 16th century the palisade was replaced by a stone curtain wall with a stone-built gatehouse. Anti-personnel cannon were installed. On the landward side of the ditch was a 'castle town' village, the sort of settlement that flourished beside such

towers. This consisted of a cluster of wattle buildings with thatched roofs, comprising stables, barns and workshops. This village was probably also defended by an outer ditch.

At the Battle of Sauchieburn in 1488 William Hay, third Earl of Erroll, and other supporters abandoned James III of Scotland to his fate. The Hays switched their support to the new king, James IV. In 1513, the Hays (87 gentlemen all bearing the same surname) were all killed at the Battle of Flodden along with James IV.

In 1594, both Old Slains Castle and the Hay residence of Delgatie Castle were destroyed under James VI's personal supervision, as a punishment for the Hays' involvement in a Catholic Spanish plot. Earlier, the Hays had been suspected of complicity in the Spanish Armada. James VI was furious at this, as it endangered his chances of achieving the English throne. Francis Hay, the ninth Earl of Erroll, wisely fled the country. When he returned three years later, he decided to rebuild Bowness Castle to the north of Old Slains – and named it New Slains.

New Slains also stands commandingly on the sea-cliffs. The 20th earl of Erroll was forced by death duties to sell the castle in 1916. Unfortunately, the new owner did not maintain it and it was finally unroofed for safety reasons in 1925, turning it instantly into a modern ruin. Bram Stoker had Slains in mind for the vampire's home when he wrote *Dracula*; Stoker often stayed in Cruden Bay nearby.

During the Armada fiasco, in which the Hays were involved as conspirators, many Spanish ships were wrecked along the coastline of Scotland and Ireland. Some of the wrecks were caused by attempts to moor close inshore in order to warn Scottish and Irish lords friendly to the Catholic cause not to invade England, because it was not safe to do so; the duke of Parma's troops, an invasion army 20,000 strong, had failed to reach England.

One galleon was wrecked off Tantallon Castle while their masters were trying to make contact with the 'Red' Douglas, and another near St Andrews Castle, though it is not known who the Spanish were trying to contact there. Another was wrecked off Old Slains Castle while trying to warn the Hays. The garrison at Old Slains must have had a clear view of this galleon as it foundered nearby. Whether the Hays sent any boats out to save the drowning sailors is not recorded, but it is unlikely that they could have done anything as the storm that blew up was sudden and severe. All three vessels were wrecked at the same time. Curiously, the 'Red' Douglas, Archibald the eighth earl of Angus, died on the same night.

The fact that the Hays of Erroll and the Gordons of Huntly were ready to come out in open rebellion against King James VI implies that they expected strong support from elsewhere. They perhaps had reason to suppose that the Spanish were about to intervene; in fact they may have been party to a conspiracy of the same type as the Spanish Armada, where an invasion was planned to coincide with a rebellion. But no Spanish ships appeared and the Hays and the Gordons lost their castles in the gamble. In fact it was not until three years later, in 1597, that the Armada was ready to sail. This time 84 mostly new galleons were assembled in Galicia. But the Hays had lost Old Slains and there was no possibility of their having anything further to do with a Spanish invasion. The Spanish had proved so unreliable and so incompetent that they could no longer rely on any help from within Britain, and because of that there could be no invasion.

Slains Castle today is a slightly unsettling place. It comes as little surprise to discover that Bram Stoker, who stayed at the castle, used it as inspiration for his story *Dracula*.

BALMORAL CASTLE

LOCATION ABERDEENSHIRE, SCOTLAND

DATE BUILT 1855

FOUNDER QUEEN VICTORIA

Following a holiday visit to Scotland which she greatly enjoyed in 1842, Queen Victoria decided to take out a lease on the small Deeside castle of Balmoral as a holiday home. Rather surprisingly, she took the little castle on without having set eyes on it.

The queen saw Balmoral for the first time six years later and was very pleased with it. She described it as 'a pretty little castle in the old Scottish style' and 'the finest I have seen anywhere', which were odd comments in view of what was to happen next.

The castle Victoria stayed in initially was an early-19th-century mansion which had been raised after the Earl of Fife had bought the estate in 1798. This mansion which Victoria so admired was designed by an Aberdeen architect by the name of John Smith. Before that, the Balmoral estate had been the property of Sir Robert Gordon and his descendants and before that it had belonged to the Farquharsons of Inverey. An even earlier castle had stood on the site, a small Scottish stone tower house that was built in about 1390 by Sir William Drummond, though it seems not to have been mentioned in any records until 1484.

But the chequered history of Balmoral Castle was not over with the arrival of Queen Victoria in 1848. She had a large family and she and Prince Albert soon found the attractive little mansion 'too small' for their needs. Prince Albert bought the freehold of Balmoral from the trustees of Sir Robert Gordon as a present for Victoria in 1852, at a cost of £31,000. It came with a substantial shooting and fishing estate amounting to 11,000 acres.

Now that they owned it, the Queen and Prince Albert could do as they liked with it. They had the house knocked down and a completely new, and of course bigger, house built 100 metres away. The site of the old house is marked by a stone. Prince Albert had a

major role in designing the new house, which was in the fashionable neo-gothic Scottish baronial style, complete with gables, towers, turrets and crenellations. It has to be said that the proportions of Albert's Balmoral leave a lot to be desired. The great tower, which stands massively to attention at one end is top-heavy with bartizans – too massive and just far too big for the rest of the house. It is joined to the rest of the house by what seems in comparison a grotesquely low range. The main block is, in itself, very well designed, picturesque and well-proportioned; it would look far better without its great tower looming 30 metres (98 ft) high beside it, even though there are some fine views from the top. The main façade is imposing and built in the local grey granite, which makes an excellent building stone.

Memorial cairns to various members of the royal family have been raised on a nearby mountain, called Craig Gowan. The new and thoroughly Victorian Balmoral Castle, the Balmoral we see today, was completed in 1855. It remained one of Queen Victoria's favourite houses for the rest of her life and she went on staying there after Prince Albert's death. She loved Balmoral and she loved Scotland too, describing it as 'the proudest, finest country in the world'.

When she became a reclusive widow, she divided her time between Balmoral and Osborne, which Albert had also helped to design. Victoria wrote adoringly of both Balmoral and her husband, 'My dearest Albert's own creation, own work, own building, own laying out.'

Prince Albert laid out the gardens and grounds near the house. The Duke of Edinburgh, the consort of the present queen, has continued this tradition by enlarging the flower and vegetable garden and creating a water garden. It was not just Queen Victoria who loved Balmoral. Successive kings and queens since Victoria have also loved it – not least

Balmoral Castle has remained a favourite residence for the queen and her family during the summer. It is part of the Balmoral Estate, a working estate which aims to protect the environment while contributing to the local economy.

because of the sense of freedom and privacy it gives, so precious to those who live their lives constantly in the public eye. The castle is around 250 metres above sea level, 'away from it all'. It is possible, even in these times of constant press intrusion, for the royal family to walk, fish, shoot and picnic on the estate at Balmoral without any thought of being watched. It is not surprising that the present queen enjoys her annual family holiday at Balmoral each August.

The estate is now five times larger than when Queen Victoria acquired it, and it employs about 50 full-time and 100 part-time staff. The estate is privately owned and funded by the queen. Among the attractions to the Royal Family are the possibilities it offers for salmon fishing, grouse shooting and hill walking.

Balmoral is a castle by name, but really a country house by function. Interestingly its name is Gaelic for 'majestic dwelling', which just about sums it up. Balmoral stands 7 miles (12 km) west of Ballater and just over a mile (2 km) from Crathie church, which the queen uses when she is in residence. Crathie church was built in 1903, and replaced the old kirk built a hundred years earlier.

Another mile or so to the west stands Abergeldie Castle, another Highland royal residence. This is an ancient building that has been added to in modern times to make it more comfortable. Abergeldie Castle was used by Edward VII when Prince of Wales, while his mother stayed at Balmoral; after her death and his accession to the throne, Abergeldie became a shooting lodge.

The estate grounds, gardens and exhibitions at Balmoral are open to the public every day from the middle of April until the last day of July, so long as the royal family is not in residence. Usually the queen arrives for her holiday there in August, and then the estate is closed to visitors. There are several cottages on the estate which can be rented as holiday homes.

CRATHES CASTLE

LOCATION **ABERDEENSHIRE, SCOTLAND**

DATE BUILT **16TH CENTURY**

FOUNDER **BURNETT FAMILY**

Crathes Castle stands to the south-west of Aberdeen. The castle is an impressive L-plan tower house, built with four storeys and an attic. Though it was founded in the 16th century, a two-storey range was added in the 18th century.

Alexander Burnett of Leys began work on the castle in 1553, and it took 46 years to complete. The massive tower tapers towards the top, giving the structure greater stability and making it easier to drop missiles onto attackers. The weak point of the classic Norman square keep was its corners; it was possible to loosen stones from the corners and so destabilize the entire structure. At Crathes, the corners were rounded, to make this harder to do.

On the turnpike stair, a tripping stone was installed. This was one step set at a different height from all the rest. The residents, defending the castle, would soon become familiar with this odd step, but a newcomer to the building, an intruder, would be likely to stumble on it when attempting to run up the stair. Then it would be up to the defenders to take advantage of the fall, which could delay the invasion of the building by several valuable seconds.

The lower storeys were originally built with minimal window openings and smooth walls for defensive reasons. The upper storeys, well out of reach from ground attack were fitted with larger windows and a variety of corbelled juts and turrets. A rather incongruous two-storey range was a later addition built on in the 18th century; no attempt was made to match the style or scale of the original. A late-Victorian wing tacked on by the 11th baronet in the late 19th century was destroyed by fire in 1966 and not rebuilt.

Crathes is extremely well preserved. Its interior is embellished with portraits, oak ceilings, heraldic shields and Jacobean painted ceilings that were only uncovered in 1877. Also on display is a jewelled ivory horn, which is thought to have been given to the Burnetts by Robert the Bruce when he granted them the Lands of Leys in 1323.

In 1951 Sir James Burnett of Leys handed over Crathes Castle and its land to the National Trust for Scotland, together with an upkeep endowment.

BRAEMAR CASTLE

LOCATION **ABERDEENSHIRE, SCOTLAND**

DATE BUILT **1628**

FOUNDER **EARL OF MAR**

John Erskine, Earl of Mar, High Treasurer of Scotland and guardian of James VI (James I of England), built his castle at Braemar in a strategically sensitive position, where the road from the pass to the south descends into the Dee valley.

The earl's neighbours, the Farquharson clan, had for a long time been enemies of the Erskines. Sixty years after Braemar was built, Grahame of Claverhouse, known as 'Bonnie Dundee', raised the Stuart standard. The Earl of Mar made no move to join him and John Farquharson, a fiery Jacobite known as 'The Black Colonel', used this as an excuse to set fire to Braemar Castle to prevent it falling to government forces. It was in ruins for over 50 years.

In the Jacobite rising of 1715, another Earl of Mar had supported the Stuarts, and as a punishment for this his Deeside estates were confiscated. In 1732 the burnt-out shell of Braemar Castle was sold to the Farquharson family who had destroyed it, and they leased it to the government. Following the 1745 rebellion, the government established strong points round the Highlands to prevent any further rebellion. They restored Braemar Castle and installed a garrison. In 1807 the Farquharsons regained possession.

Braemar Castle is built as a conventional L-plan tower house, five storeys tall, with a large newel staircase built in the angle to give easy access to rooms in both wings on each level. Despite the corner cylindrical turrets being too tall and too bulky, the overall design of the castle is of great architectural interest because it shows very well the style of the later tower houses.

When the Hanoverian government leased the castle in 1748, the architect charged with restoring it was John Adam. He heightened the staircase tower and bartizans, replacing their conical tiled roofs with flat battlemented tops that were more practical in terms of 18th-century warfare. Adam also added a curtain wall round the castle, with six sharp-angled projections provided with gun-slits that were designed to cover the approaches. The exterior is rather bleak, but the scale of the interior is cosy and intimate; it is a castle that would be pleasant to live in, with attractive views across meadows to the River Dee.

GLAMIS CASTLE

LOCATION **ANGUS, SCOTLAND**

DATE BUILT **11TH CENTURY**

FOUNDER **KINGS OF SCOTLAND**

Glamis (pronounced 'Glahms') was built in the 11th century as a royal hunting lodge for the Scottish kings. The name comes from the Gaelic *glamhus*, or vale.

William Shakespeare famously set the murder of King Duncan I at Glamis in his Scottish play, but Shakespeare was using a great deal of dramatic licence. Duncan was not murdered there; in fact he was not murdered in his sleep at all, but died in battle. He did, however, meet his death in 1040, fighting against Macbeth, who was a rival claimant to the Scottish throne. Duncan's predecessor and maternal grandfather, King Malcolm II, is believed to have died there in 1034. Several later Scottish kings were to live at Glamis.

When the poet Thomas Gray stayed there in 1765 he wrote that it was 'very singular and striking in appearance, like nothing I ever saw'. The first sight the visitor sees, framed at the end of a long and wide avenue of oak trees, is a massive and high building bristling with clusters of pointed turrets. The effect of loftiness and mass would have been enhanced before the wings lost their gabled roofs. Around the year 1800 the old gabled roofs were taken off to give them a crenellated roofline, and this was a mistake; pitched roofs with gables would harmonize better with the pointed turrets and spires.

The castle is in any case a splendid example of the Scottish baronial style, an amalgam of the Scottish tower house and the French Renaissance chateau. With its 17th-century battlements, corner turrets and conical spires it comes closer than almost any other building in Britain to a fairytale castle. The decorative details that give it such a distinctive skyline probably did nothing for the castle's defensive capacity, but at the core of Glamis is a stout, no-nonsense 14th-century tower, which makes it a real castle. A 14th-century iron yett (latticed wrought-iron gate) still defends the main entrance; this device is a massive grille that replaced the portcullis.

The core of the castle dates from the 14th and 15th centuries, at which time
it was surrounded by a curtain wall. In the 17th century it was remodelled, and the
interior was decorated with fine plasterwork. It was after the Restoration that the
third Earl of Strathmore and Kinghorne heightened the main block and gave it its
fancy roofline.

In 1372, the castle passed to Sir John Lyon. When he married the daughter
of King Robert II, his grandson became the first Lord Glamis. In the 16th century
the castle was seized by James V, who took all its contents and ensured that Lady
Glamis was burnt as a witch. There was no evidence against her, but she was a
Douglas, and that was enough to make the king hate her. She was executed on
Castle Hill in 1540. It was one of the most outstandingly scandalous, cruel and
unjust acts in a century that excelled in scandal, cruelty and injustice.

In the 17th century the Lords of Glamis acquired the earldoms of Kinghorne
and Strathmore. The fifth earl was a close friend and follower of Montrose. The
family's Stuart sympathies lingered on, and the Stuart heir to the throne of England

and Scotland, who was known to the English as 'The Old Pretender', and to his followers as the Chevalier de St George or even James VIII, was entertained at Glamis Castle. Relics of the king-in-exile are still kept at the castle, including his coat, breeches, sword and watch. These 18th-century Lords of Glamis lived in ostentatiously high style. It seems they were the very last aristocratic family in Scotland to maintain a court jester. The last jester's silken suit of motley has been preserved.

In 1767, the family made a great fortune for itself when the ninth earl married the Durham heiress Mary Bowes; from then on the family was known as Bowes Lyon. Glamis is one of the finest private houses in Britain and it holds a special place in the affections of the British because it was where the queen mother spent her childhood, her honeymoon and where she gave birth to her second daughter, Princess Margaret.

Glamis is said to be the most haunted castle in the British Isles. The Grey Lady, who has been seen from time to time, is said to be the ghost of Janet Douglas who was burnt at the stake in the 16th century. Another ghost is that of a page-boy. He was apparently told to sit on the step and wait until the family was ready for him; he was then completely forgotten about and just went on sitting there. He is said to be sitting there still, tripping up passers-by for fun.

Glamis has a secret chamber, but only the castle's owner knows where it is. There is even a ghost story to explain why the chamber cannot be found. One evening the Earl of Glamis and his friend were playing cards in a room in the castle. Late in the evening a page went to warn them that midnight approached and that it would be a sin to continue playing on into the sabbath. Apparently they went on playing regardless and at midnight the walls of the chamber sealed around them like a tomb. The ghosts of the earl and his friend are said to go on and on

playing cards; around midnight the sound of their game can still be heard.

Modern visitors, who naturally never visit the secret chamber, see the dining room first, a rare and unexpected example of untouched 19th-century decor – in Elizabethan style. It contrasts dramatically with the barrel-vaulted crypt that lies beyond, its plain walls set with hunting trophies and weapons. Over the crypt is the Jacobean great hall, which is now called the drawing room.

The suite of royal apartments was arranged by the 14th Countess of Strathmore for her youngest daughter when the latter was Duchess of York; the duchess continually returned to these apartments as duchess, then as Queen Elizabeth, and then as Queen Elizabeth the Queen Mother.

CLAYPOTTS CASTLE

LOCATION **CITY OF DUNDEE**
DATE BUILT **16TH CENTURY**
FOUNDER **STRACHAN FAMILY**

**The home of the Strachan family near Dundee is a typical
example of a post-Reformation tower house. At Claypotts
it is easy to see how these structures got their name. This
really is a house hoisted up on top of a tower.**

After the 16th-century Reformation in Scotland, when the age of castles was
all but over, more modest fortified houses were built by lairds who owned
just one modest estate. Even before the Reformation, the Strachans were lay
tenants of land belonging to three abbeys. For their main holding, which
was Claypotts, they paid an annual rent of £12 and 12 cockerels. After the
Reformation, the Strachans' hold on the land was strengthened and John
Strachan embarked on a new building that would reflect his new status.

The structure, which has the date 1569 carved on it, was built on what
is sometimes described as a Z-plan, with two massive round towers projecting
from opposite corners of the main block. Twelve gunholes puncture the walls
down at ground level, which are obviously there to enable the Strachans to
shoot down marauders. These and other features, however, are not so much
military as domestic; the Strachans were really only keeping out burglars.

Claypotts, which is extremely well preserved, was similar to earlier
tower houses, only with some refinements. Two staircases were provided, one
for the gentlefolk and one for the servants and the sanitation was improved.
This tower house was built right at the end of the castle tradition; it had
become refined into a comfortable lord's residence. John Strachan's will, made
in the 1590s, shows that he was not rich, but a cut above the average farmer.

Claypotts was an influential castle. When King James VI of Scotland
organized the colonization of Ulster, Scottish gentlemen went to Ireland and
built themselves tower houses on the Scottish model; thus Monea Castle in
County Fermanagh looks remarkably like Claypotts.

The most distinctive feature of Claypotts is the way the round towers
are corbelled out to bear rectangular 'cap houses' on top, looking for all the
world like a pair of humble farm cottages hoisted up on big round pillars.

KILCHURN CASTLE

LOCATION **ARGYLL & BUTE, SCOTLAND**
DATE BUILT *c.* 1420
FOUNDER **SIR COLIN CAMPBELL**

Today, Kilchurn Castle is an imposing valley floor ruin standing on a little peninsula on the marshy banks of Loch Awe. What we see represents 250 years of thoughtful building and occupation, followed by 250 years of abandonment and neglect.

It was in about 1420 that Sir Colin Campbell of Glenorchy first built the five-storey tower house which still stands intact at the eastern end of the site. The tower house was the standard design for a Scottish fortified home, the equivalent of the English moated manor house. It was quite common for English castles to be entered at first-floor level, but Kilchurn was entered from the ground floor. Immediately above the vaulted entrance hall was the great hall, with two further storeys stacked above it to provide accommodation. At the top of the castle was an attic or garret leading out onto a parapet walk. A curtain wall, sometimes called a barmkin wall, enclosed the rest of the site; the southern stretch of this is still standing.

Early in the 16th century Kilchurn Castle was extended by Sir Duncan Campbell, who added a single-storey dining hall up against the inside of the south curtain wall. His descendant, another Sir Colin, the sixth Laird of Kilchurn, added some chambers to the north of the tower house and remodelled the parapet; this included adding some round corner turrets with stone corbels, which are still in position. At the end of the 16th century the MacGregors of Glenstrae were the occupants of the castle; they were appointed keepers of Kilchurn when the Campbells spent much of their time at Fincham. This amicable arrangement lasted until the early 17th century, when a violent feud between the two families brought it to an end.

Once an imposing tower house, Kilchurn Castle is now an atmospheric ruin standing beside Loch Awe.

In 1616 the seventh Laird of Kilchurn, Sir Duncan, added a second storey to the dining hall and extended it to join the tower house. This extension included space for a chapel. The final stage in the castle's development was the building of a range of barracks along the northern curtain wall. At the same time three round towers were added to strengthen the north, south and west corners of the curtain wall; two of these are still standing.

Kilchurn is one of those castles that by chance had a fairly trouble-free history. The only significant military incident was in 1685, when it briefly came under siege. It was garrisoned by Sir John, the first Earl of Breadalbane, while he was supporting the government against the Earl of Argyll's invasion. Kilchurn Castle was again garrisoned by government troops during later insurrections, the 1715 and 1745 Jacobite Rebellions. By that stage, the castle had been virtually abandoned by its owners, who moved to Taymouth Castle in 1740. That spelt the end for Kilchurn.

The castle quickly fell into a state of decay. First abandoned by its family, then struck by lightning in 1769 and losing its roof in 1770, the hostile elements did not take long to turn this carefully crafted fortress into a ruin.

IONA ABBEY

LOCATION ARGYLL & BUTE, SCOTLAND

DATE BUILT 563

FOUNDER ST COLUMBA

Iona is the site of the most important early monastery in Scotland, founded in 563 by the Irish missionary St Columba. It was a day's sail away from Ireland – and a springboard for the conversion of Scotland to the Christian faith.

The foundation of Iona marked the beginning of a continuous tradition of Christianity and monasticism in Scotland. The most impressive remains at this major site are of an earthwork which defines the roughly rectangular precinct. This was a dynamic and flourishing early Christian community, as is shown by the magnificent high crosses. Many early Scottish kings wanted to be buried at what came to be regarded as an exceptionally holy place.

The medieval abbey of Iona was a much later development, but it was built upon the same site as the historic monastery. Most of the original abbey church has gone, but the details of the contemporary Augustinian nunnery nearby show what it was probably like. The arcades flanking the nave were rounded Romanesque arches. The windows were round-headed and splayed and linked by prominent string courses in the masonry. The design was essentially in a Romanesque style borrowed more from Ireland than from Scotland. The founder of both the abbey and the nunnery was Reginald, the son of Somerled, the King of the Isles. He founded Iona Abbey in about 1200.

The church and abbey are complete, but much of what is seen today at Iona is a result of modern restoration. Even so, the chancel and the south transept are still essentially the same as when they were remodelled in the later middle ages; the north transept has survived from the earlier building period. The remodelling involved destroying a crypt and lowering the floor level of the choir and presbytery; it also involved shortening the north aisle to make a sacristy. A new, squat tower was built over the crossing. The result is a well-proportioned, compact and serviceable building.

The abbey of Iona was restored in recent times specifically for the Iona Community. It has become, once again, a focus for pilgrimage, as people come from all over the world to a place that seems to have a special sanctity.

INVERARAY CASTLE

LOCATION **ARGYLL & BUTE, SCOTLAND**
DATE BUILT **18TH CENTURY**
FOUNDER **ARCHIBALD, THIRD DUKE OF ARGYLL**

Inveraray Castle on Loch Fyne is the home of the Dukes of Argyll and its story is inextricably intertwined with theirs. As the present duke, Torquhil, the 13th Duke, has said, Inveraray Castle is first and foremost a family home.

The Campbells have been Earls of Argyll since 1457. The tenth earl was a vigorous anti-Jacobite and champion of William of Orange. For this he was raised to the dukedom in 1701. The Argylls' ancient stronghold was Innischonnel Castle, now a ruin, on Loch Awe.

In 1743, however, the third duke, Archibald, launched one of the most ambitious building projects ever seen in the Highlands of Scotland. There was a 15th-century fortified tower house at Inveraray, so he replaced it with an entirely new castle. The walls were up and the roof on within ten years. It was all completed by the time of Dr Johnson's visit in 1773. The old settlement of Inveraray, which lay across the present garden, was rebuilt further away.

Inveraray Castle is an extraordinary building. It stands foursquare and moatless, with graceful conical spires rising from round corner towers. The façade is pure French chateau, but peeping over its roofline is a more rugged, battlemented superstructure that is at odds with the civilized façade. It breaks across, as if to remind us of a barbaric past. But overall Inveraray is a great house, a rich mansion. The interior reinforces this impression, though in classical style, not Gothic. There is a fine Victorian room, while the clan room is devoted to telling the story of the development of the Clan Campbell.

The castle was designed by the London architect Roger Morris, and the supervising architects were William and John Adam. Morris was an odd choice, as he was not a 'palace' man, though he had designed Clearwell Castle in Gloucestershire. Duke Archibald's castle was not at all Scottish; it was low, urbane, civilized and convenient. The strange architecture is perfectly matched by the choice of building stone, a greenish-blue schist, which gives an otherworldly look to the building. The magnificent interiors were designed by Robert Mylne for the fifth duke at the time of the French Revolution.

ST ANDREWS CATHEDRAL & CASTLE

LOCATION **FIFE, SCOTLAND**

DATE BUILT **1160 (CATHEDRAL); 14TH CENTURY (CASTLE)**

FOUNDER **BISHOPS OF ST ANDREWS**

St Andrews was a monastery and the seat of a bishop at least as early as the eighth century, when Bishop Acca was exiled from his diocese at Hexham and settled here.

The bishop brought with him the relics of St Andrew that gave the place its new name of Kinrimund. The bishops of St Andrews emerged as the most important in Scotland, calling themselves Bishops of the Scots.

The cathedral that was started in 1160 is in a very ruined state, but enough fragments survive to show what at least the eastern part must have looked like. An attractive feature is the intersecting arcading along the transept walls, consisting of two sets of round arches following each other. It was here that features such as piers made of bundles of shafts and leaf-form capitals were first used in a major Scottish church. The east gable wall stands intact, but with no walls attached on either side, making it look rather odd. A substantial part of the west front still standing, but nothing much in between.

As the Reformation approached, signs of decadence began to appear. In 1513, the Archbishop of St Andrews, James IV's illegitimate son, was killed at Flodden. The pope hoped to impose his own nephew, but the Scots had strong ideas of their own. Further confusion followed soon after when Henry VIII of England rejected the pope as head of the English church.

It was common for Scottish bishops to have their own castles. The Archbishop of St Andrews lived in a castle that was built in about 1200, destroyed, and then rebuilt by Bishop Walter Trail in the 14th century. Trail laid his castle out as an irregular pentagon with towers at the angles and ranges of buildings against the curtain walls. It made a formidable stronghold. But even the strongest castle could not defend a bishop against a determined siege – or against assassination. The nephew of Archbishop James Beaton, Cardinal David Beaton, was murdered in St Andrews Castle in 1546 and the castle was afterwards taken following bombardment by a French fleet.

STIRLING CASTLE

LOCATION **STIRLING, SCOTLAND**

DATE BUILT **15TH CENTURY (ON SITE OF EARLIER CASTLE)**

FOUNDER **KING JAMES III OF SCOTLAND**

When Edward I of England invaded, Stirling Castle was reckoned to be the strongest fortress in Scotland. It was still mainly timber, yet it withstood the onslaught of the English stone-throwing engines so well that Edward was reduced to stripping the lead from cathedral roofs in order to increase the power of his catapults.

Unfortunately all trace of the castle as it was at the time of the Battle of Bannockburn in 1314 has disappeared. It was James III of Scotland (1460–88) who gave Stirling Castle its commanding dignity by giving it a central turreted gatehouse, curtain walls and flanking towers. Directly opposite the gatehouse he had a great hall built where parliaments and state ceremonies could be held.

Stirling Castle has an unusual layout. On the south-east side is the counterguard, an area of outer defensive works consisting of walls, ditches and gun batteries. On the north-west side is the nether bailey, an enclosure with no buildings in it. Between the two is the castle proper, which consists of a palace block on the south side and three major buildings, the great hall, the king's old building and the chapel royal, arranged round an open space, the upper square.

In April 1304, after wintering at Dunfermline, Edward I began his great siege of Stirling Castle. The defenders under Sir William Oliphant held out for three months without any real hope of being relieved. The castle itself was impregnable, but the garrison had to surrender in the end because they ran out of food. In July, Oliphant and his followers marched out and were sent off to various English prisons. For the next ten years, Stirling Castle stood as a symbol of English authority, blocking communication between north and south.

In 1313, the castle came under a blockade by Edward Bruce, the brother of King Robert. Sir Philip Mowbray, the English custodian, offered to surrender if relief had not come by 24 June 1314. Edward Bruce agreed to

these terms, which alarmed his brother, who was not ready to meet the English in a pitched battle.

Edward II marched north with a huge feudal army, drawing up in sight of Stirling Castle. He sent a detachment to help the castle garrison, but this was driven back. Against all expectation, the Scots then defeated the huge English host on the nearby field of Bannockburn. The castle was surrendered to the Scots as promised, and then Robert the Bruce set about dismantling its fortifications in case the English reoccupied them, which they did shortly afterwards.

With the Stewarts on the throne, Stirling Castle once more became a royal residence. James II made the castle a dower-house for his queen, Mary, and when they were married a magnificent tournament was held below the castle walls. In 1452, James II formed the idea that William Earl of Douglas was plotting against him. He invited Douglas to Stirling,

Stone towers punctuate the outer curtain wall of this strongly defended castle.

promising him safe conduct. Douglas arrived and was cordially entertained at dinner. Then the king invited Douglas to an inner chamber to confer. In this brief discussion James II asked Douglas to dissolve the league of Douglas and Douglas said that he could not or would not. In James's mind the survival of the monarchy depended on the removal of this powerful league, and he promptly stabbed the earl. James's courtiers sprang forward to make sure the earl was dead, and his body was flung out of the window. An enquiry into the murder acquitted the king on the grounds that the earl had been an oppressor and had refused to aid the king. These findings only fanned rebellion, and the dead earl's brother, James, the new ninth earl, rode up to Stirling Castle brandishing the letter of safe conduct.

James IV, who acquired the throne by rebelling against and killing his father in 1488, indulged his guilt at Stirling. He spent a lot of time in the chapel royal and 'was ever sad and dolorous in his mind for the death of his father'. But James IV had his lighter side. He enjoyed hunting and ensured that the royal castle garden, known as the great garden or the king's knot, was well maintained. He had a new park stocked with deer, boars and wild white cattle. Cranes and peacocks stalked the castle precincts. It was the peak of Stirling Castle's medieval splendour.

James IV's alliance with France against England brought him into conflict with the Tudor kings of England. In April 1513 an envoy from Henry VIII arrived at Stirling Castle to try to persuade James IV to abandon his alliance with France. He refused, and five months later he spectacularly lost the Battle of Flodden – and his life.

It was at Stirling Castle that the young Mary Queen of Scots was crowned. Henry VIII's envoy acidly commented that the coronation was conducted 'with such solemnity as they do use in this country, which is not very costly'. Mary later used Stirling

Castle as a stopping place on journeys north. One night when she was in bed at Stirling she set her bed curtains on fire with a candle and she was nearly overcome by the smoke. In 1566 an elaborate baptism was celebrated for her infant son, to be James VI of Scotland, costing £12,000. Expensive gifts lavished on the child included a gold font from Elizabeth I, Prince James's godmother. Torches lined the way from the nursery to the chapel, where an archbishop and four bishops waited to perform the ceremony.

After the murder of his father and the forced abdication of his mother, the one-year-old James was crowned King James VI at Stirling, and kept under protection in Stirling Castle while the great lords struggled for power around him. In due course James VI laid on another expensive baptism, for his own son, Prince Henry. This ceremony cost the Scots £100,000 and took place in the rebuilt chapel royal. Prince Henry was the last Prince of Scotland to be brought up at Stirling Castle. Once the crowns of Scotland

ABOVE Its imposing position means that Stirling Castle commands the surrounding countryside. It towers over some important battlefields, including Stirling Bridge, the site of William Wallace's victory over the English in 1297, and Bannockburn.

and England were united, the glory of Stirling Castle instantly evaporated.

In the Civil War, General Monk bombarded Stirling Castle for three days in August 1651 and caused a great deal of damage. The castle was ransacked by the Parliamentarians, who took wall-hangings and 40 guns.

After the Restoration of the monarchy in 1660, the castle was returned to the Earl of Mar, though it was taken from his family by the English Crown at the time of the Jacobite rebellions when it was suspected of disloyalty. Curiously, in 1923, Stirling Castle was restored to the Earl of Mar by George V.

TANTALLON CASTLE

LOCATION **EAST LOTHIAN, SCOTLAND**
DATE BUILT *c.* **1358**
FOUNDER **WILLIAM, FIRST EARL OF DOUGLAS**

Sir James Douglas was a close friend of Robert the Bruce and the rise of the Douglas fortunes, including their acquisition of estates throughout Scotland, was the fruit of this friendship. Tantallon was one such estate.

When Sir James Douglas died in 1330, his heir was his nephew William, who built the powerful Tantallon Castle. He probably built it to mark his elevation to the peerage as the first Earl of Douglas in 1358.

Tantallon Castle stands impressively atop vertical cliffs, which provide natural defence on two sides. On the other two sides, to landward, are lines of ditches and walls, defining two courts or baileys. The inner court is shielded by an awesome red sandstone curtain wall, which dates from the very first building phase; it rears up behind a yawning rock-cut ditch.

The oddly isolated dovecote that stands forlornly in the middle of the outer ward belongs to the final phase of the castle's history as a lordly residence in the 17th century. In between, Tantallon Castle served as a major fortress-residence of the Douglases for 400 years.

The massive curtain wall has three ruined towers projecting from it, providing the main residential accommodation. The north tower, the Douglas Tower, is a mighty and impressive building, rising seven storeys. This was certainly the earl's dwelling. Immediately behind it is a two-storey block with a great hall on the upper floor, reserved for the use of the lord and his family.

In the 16th century, Tantallon and Craignethan were the only lordly residences in Scotland to have artillery fortifications incorporated into their structures. Tantallon was badly damaged by James V's bombardment in 1528; afterwards the structure was patched with green stone. In the Civil War of the 17th century an attempt was made to improve Tantallon's fortifications by adding triangular earthwork gun emplacements called ravelins.

Tantallon was a quite exceptional castle. At this time most were opting for less ambitious residences and William himself built more modestly at another of his properties, but at Tantallon he made a flamboyant gesture.

EDINBURGH CASTLE

LOCATION **CITY OF EDINBURGH, SCOTLAND**
DATE BUILT *c.* **1130 (ON SITE OF EARLIER CASTLE)**
FOUNDER **KING DAVID I OF SCOTLAND**

Edinburgh is dominated by its castle like few other cities. At just over 100 metres (330 ft) high, its Castle Rock is not especially high, yet it provides the ideal location for an early medieval stronghold.

From the summit there are wide views across the Lowlands of Scotland, and its near-vertical rocky crags make it the ideal defensive site. The castle was built on the highest point of a crag-and-tail, a stream-lined feature eroded by ice, and the tail gives a single gently sloping access route, Edinburgh's main street, the Royal Mile.

Edinburgh Castle was the core of the original settlement. Indeed, back in the dark ages, one and a half millennia ago, the fortress on the rock was the sum total of the settlement. It was called Din Eiddyn. It seems that as early as the sixth century AD, and possibly earlier, Castle Rock was a royal stronghold. Only a few archaeological traces remain of this early phase of occupation; the original stronghold has been obliterated by later developments on the rock. During the middle ages a town grew up outside its gates, which became the Royal Mile, the core of the old city of Edinburgh.

Within Edinburgh Castle are rooms associated with various Scottish kings and queens. The oldest of these chambers is the small chapel of Queen Margaret (or St Margaret), who died in 1093 shortly after her husband Malcolm III (Malcolm Canmore). The nave is 4 metres (13 ft) long and the chancel less than 3 metres (10 ft).

There is a decorated Norman arch leading
to an apse that is, unusually, semicircular
inside but square outside.

Beside the chapel is the famous
Mons Meg, a huge 15th-century bombard
or cannon, weighing 5 tonnes; it fired
cannonballs 50 cm (19½ in) in diameter.

Beyond the high rock where the chapel
stands is the bastion of the Half-Moon
Battery. This overlooks the steep slope
down into Princes Street Gardens towards
a distant view of the Firth of Forth. Close
by is Crown Square, and on the east side of
this square is the 16th-century royal lodging
containing the Crown Room where the
Scottish crown jewels lie in a glass case: the
crown, sceptre, sword of state and other
jewels belonging to the kings and queens of
Scotland – the Honours of Scotland. There
are also the apartments of Mary of Guise
and her daughter, Mary Queen of Scots,
including a tiny bedroom lit by an oriel
window; on its ceiling are many painted
monograms of Mary Queen of Scots and her
son, James VI, who was born there in 1566.

On the south side of the square is the
15th-century banqueting hall, which was
restored in 1888. On the west side of the
square is the Naval and Military Museum,
with relics of various Scots regiments. On
the north side is the Scottish National
Memorial, in effect a war memorial, which
stands on the site of the 12th-century church
of St Mary.

BORTHWICK CASTLE

LOCATION **MIDLOTHIAN, SCOTLAND**

DATE BUILT **1430**

FOUNDER **SIR WILLIAM BORTHWICK**

Of all the tower houses built in Scotland in the 15th century, Borthwick Castle is the one that stands out as truly exceptional, being the tallest and the largest in scale.

Borthwick is also the most sophisticated architecturally, with high-quality ashlar masonry and cleverly arranged accommodation. It represents the climax in the development of that particular type of castle.

It was in 1420 that Sir William Borthwick was granted his licence 'to construct a castle . . . and fortify the same'. Sir William must have been very proud of his castle, which was so far in advance of any other. He must also have been the envy of his peers, although he was only in the second rank of the nobility at the time when he built it; it was 20 years before he was raised to the peerage by James II, and given the title Lord Borthwick.

Sir William's design at Borthwick seems to have been driven not just by a desire to impress but by a desire to pull all of the accommodation into a single massive tower under a single roof. The plan is a kind of E-plan with the central stem missing, or a cube with a slot cut into one side; the walls rise sheer to a level roofline on all sides, giving each floor the same outline plan. The ground and first floors consisted of store rooms, a prison and a steward's chamber. The second floor housed a magnificent and impressive great hall with a soaring 10-metre-high stone vault. Leading off it were kitchens on one side and a withdrawing chamber on the other. The floors above that consisted of the lord's apartments, which included a further hall and a chapel.

A curiosity of Borthwick Castle is the many masons' marks cut into the ashlar blocks. These were symbols carved into the blocks to indicate which part of the building they were intended for. There are over 60 different marks at Borthwick and, among other things, they show that the castle was built all in one go. The spiral staircases and even the kerb on the well in the basement all turn out to be part of the original design. The marks also show that several additional masons were brought in to work on the massive vaulted ceiling for the great hall, which was intended to be a spectacular set piece.

MELROSE ABBEY

LOCATION **SCOTTISH BORDERS, SCOTLAND**

DATE BUILT **1136**

FOUNDER **KING DAVID I OF SCOTLAND**

King David I set about reorganizing the Scottish church with gusto. He introduced the Cistercians to Scotland at Melrose in 1136. Benefactors set up funds for treats, such as the one Robert I gave to Melrose in 1326 to allow the monks a daily helping of rice made with milk of almonds.

One of the specialities of Melrose, as at several other abbeys, was wool production. Melrose sent its wool to the Low Countries; in fact Melrose Abbey was the biggest single producer of wool in Scotland and gained special privileges from the Court of Flanders in the 1180s.

Melrose had to be rebuilt after the English attacked it in 1385, and the rebuilding was done under the authority of the English king, Richard II, who provided funding for the work. Probably he regarded southern Scotland as reconquered by this stage. The new Melrose was laid out as a larger version of the old. The quality of the new work was outstandingly high, lavishly enriched with sculpted decoration. An English mason was responsible for the window tracery, where the English Perpendicular style is visible; verticals rise through the full height of the windows. Then there is a change, and in the south transept window the verticals veer to make flowing tracery patterns; by the early years of the 15th century, the masons at Melrose were looking to Europe for inspiration. In fact, a French mason included two inscriptions telling us that he was called John Morow and that he had been born in Paris. But the ambitious rebuilding launched by Richard II was never completed.

In 1556, the abbey church was becoming unusable through neglect. There was a long period of deterioration. Fittings disappeared or were allocated to other churches, including choir stalls originating from Bruges.

The outlines of all the main buildings at Melrose Abbey have been revealed through excavation. There are also some fine stretches of wall standing to full height to give a good impression of the building in its heyday. The abbey church as seen from the south-east is spectacular. Overall, Melrose is the most beautiful of all the ruins in Scotland.

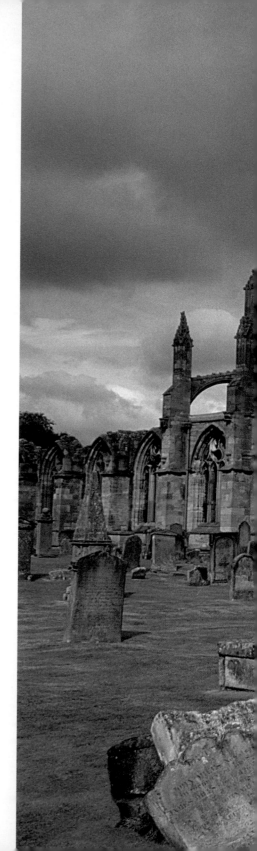

DRYBURGH ABBEY

LOCATION **SCOTTISH BORDERS, SCOTLAND**

DATE BUILT *c.* **1150**

FOUNDER **HUGO DE MORVILLE**

Dryburgh Abbey stands south-east of Melrose in southern Scotland. It was founded by Hugo de Morville, the Constable of Scotland, who brought a community of monks from Alnwick in Northumberland.

Dryburgh was the last of the Border Abbeys to be founded, and the only one to be created under the instructions of King David I. It was built by monks of the Premonstratensian Order, who were known as White Canons because of their white habits. They focused on a contemplative, cloistered life.

The abbey stands on a wooded promontory with the River Tweed sweeping round it on three sides. However, because this is border country, it was almost inevitable that it would become ensnared in cross-border fighting.

The layout of Dryburgh Abbey was standard – a cross-plan church with a big square tower at the crossing. The main nave was flanked by side aisles, and south of that was a large square cloister garth and a ranger of monastic buildings. The remains of Dryburgh are mostly Early English in style, but with some Norman work. Of the church itself, only fragments remain – the western gable, the ends of the transept, part of the choir – but these are of wonderful architectural quality and rich in detail. The monastic buildings have survived better, including the refectory with its beautiful rose window.

Perhaps the main point of historical interest is the tomb of Sir Walter Scott in St Mary's aisle, which is part of the north transept. Scott's mother's family, the Haliburtons, had once owned Dryburgh. Scott thought the ruins of Dryburgh were the most romantic in the world.

The abbey was first attacked by the English in 1322; Edward II camped in its grounds during his retreat from Scotland and set it on fire. The buildings were restored, but there were further attacks in 1385, 1523 and 1544. Dryburgh never recovered. When the last of the canons died, the abbey was abandoned and passed into the ownership of the Earl of Mar.

In 1780, the Earl of Buchan bought Dryburgh and set about conserving the ruins. It is, as Scott said, the most perfect picturesque ruin imaginable.

JEDBURGH ABBEY

LOCATION SCOTTISH BORDERS, SCOTLAND

DATE BUILT 1138

FOUNDER KING DAVID I AND BISHOP JOHN OF GLASGOW

David I of Scotland invested a huge amount of money and energy into reinvigorating the church in Scotland. Three churches illustrate his highest architectural aspirations for the monastic church – Dunfermline, Kelso and Jedburgh abbeys – each built to serve three different monastic orders.

Jedburgh was built for the Augustinian monks. Here David built big because this was border country and he wanted to demonstrate to the English that Scottish abbeys were every bit the equal of English abbeys. The magnificent remains of Jedburgh are still overwhelmingly impressive when approached from the direction of England, just as King David intended.

Of the abbey church begun in 1138, only the western bays of the chancel and parts of the transepts survive. The most striking feature of the oldest part of the building is the way the two lower storeys of the chancel were embraced by giant arches carried on huge cylindrical piers. The effect is very beautiful indeed, especially given the bold and confident detailing on the arches. This was a design that originated in the choir of Tewkesbury Abbey in Gloucestershire. Some of the details imply that the masons working at Jedburgh may have travelled there directly from Tewkesbury.

The three-tiered arcaded nave at Jedburgh is magnificent. It has pillars that are clusters of eight shafts, rising to leaf-form capitals. The nave is 40 metres (131 ft) long and complete – except for its steeply pitched roof, and there is a clear upturned V mark on the west wall of the still-standing tower to show exactly where the absent roof should go. The north transept was doubled in size, possibly to make space for extra chapels or altars.

Jedburgh was subjected to a devastating attack by the English in the 1540s, which led to a flurry of late rebuilding activity. With the benefit of hindsight, this looks like a lost cause. But interest in keeping the building alive as a piece of architecture was still there, and an awareness dawned that stripping away modern additions might allow people to appreciate the wonders of the medieval work in an abbey that was truly a masterpiece.

SWEETHEART ABBEY

LOCATION **DUMFRIES & GALLOWAY, SCOTLAND**

DATE BUILT **1275**

FOUNDER **LADY DEVORGILLA**

Sweetheart Abbey was named by the abbey's monks in honour of the founder, Lady Devorgilla. She had the monastery built in 1275 in memory of her husband King John de Balliol.

Lady Devorgilla had her husband's embalmed heart kept there in a casket of silver and ivory. When she too died, in 1289, she was buried in front of the high altar, with her husband's heart. It was a very fine Early English church, with a central tower 28 metres (92 ft) high. The monastic buildings were on the same large scale and surrounded by an enclosure wall of granite 3 metres (10 ft) high.

Sweetheart Abbey is in border country, which put it in the path of invading English armies. In 1300, Edward I of England stayed here after sacking Caerlaverock Castle. While here he heard that there was a demand from the pope to stop his oppression of the Scots. This led to a truce and Edward's return to England late in 1300. Later, Lady Devorgilla's son John Balliol would be Edward I's nominee for the Scottish throne.

Unlike other border abbeys, Sweetheart Abbey did not suffer from the English invasions, and it continued as a place of worship – even through the Reformation. When the Lords of the Congregation ordered that the abbey must be destroyed in 1560, the sixth Lord Maxwell refused, saying that he was attached to the place where he was brought up.

Sweetheart Abbey's final years were spent under its best-known superior, Abbot Gilbert Broun, who went on upholding the Catholic faith long after the Reformation. The last monks were forced to leave Sweetheart in 1608.

Then the great abbey became a quarry for those who wanted ready-shaped stone for building. The piecemeal destruction continued for 200 years, until in the 19th century some local people acquired the property and stopped its deterioration. Thanks to this intervention, the ruins are substantial. At the red broken heart of the abbey ruins is a reminder of the love story that led to its building over 700 years ago, an effigy of Lady Devorgilla, holding the casket containing her husband's heart.

CAERLAVEROCK CASTLE

LOCATION **DUMFRIES & GALLOWAY, SCOTLAND**

DATE BUILT **13TH CENTURY**

FOUNDER **MAXWELL FAMILY**

Repeatedly in its history, this water-surrounded castle became entangled in the border conflict between England and Scotland.

In 1300, when it was but 20 years old, Caerlaverock was besieged and taken by Edward I, who then held it for 12 years until the keeper of the castle switched his allegiance to Robert the Bruce. The English returned, but this time they failed to take it. Clearly Caerlaverock was seen as an important strategic stronghold by the English, so Robert the Bruce ordered the keeper, Sir Eustace Maxwell, to dismantle it and so prevent the English from using it.

Remains of an earlier castle can be seen in the woods a few hundred metres away. The place was an important strategic point in the dark ages. Close to the head of Solway Firth, it was on the Roman road linking the two northern kingdoms of Rheged (Cumbria) and Clyde (south-west Scotland). In 573 the great Battle of Arderydd (Arthuret) was fought at Longtown.

King Gwenddolau was master of Caelaverock then, and he was one of the leading combatants who died in the battle round his own fortress. Gwenddolau had a bard like other kings, but his bard was called Myrddin, which makes us look more closely at him. Myrddin fought in the battle alongside his master. When he saw his lord killed, he went mad and became a hermit in the Wood of Celidon. Myrddin was undoubtedly the prototype for the 'Merlin' who was later alleged to have been Arthur's bard. Castles and especially ruined castles seem to attract histories and legends round their weathered stones. Warriors and wraiths are equally part of their story. Caerlaverock is especially rich in this layering of past and possibility. It is hauntingly strange to think of Merlin's historical model, Myrddin, fighting in a pitched battle under the walls of Caerlaverock Castle's predecessor. And how much stranger still to think of him running off into the woods grief-stricken and distraught, suffering from a dark age version of shell-shock.

IRELAND

DUNLUCE CASTLE

LOCATION **COLERAINE, NORTHERN IRELAND**

DATE BUILT **14TH CENTURY (ON SITE OF EARLIER CASTLE)**

FOUNDER **MCQUILLAN FAMILY**

The ruins of Dunluce Castle have a desolate grandeur, rising melodramatically from a basalt cliff, which in turn looms out of the sea.

The castle rock, which is separated from the mainland by a deep natural chasm, occupied a position of profound strategic importance. It was fought over repeatedly until in the 16th century it became the main stronghold of the McDonnells.

Dunluce was probably in use as a defensive site 2000 years ago. A souterrain, an underground storage tunnel or refuge, survives from this early period under the ruins of the later castle. The first stone castle was built in the 13th century by Richard de Burgh. The earliest surviving features of the stone castle are the two big round towers 9 metres (29½ ft) in diameter on the east side. These are remnants of the castle built in the 14th century by the McQuillans after they became lords of 'The Route', as the area was known.

Most of the stonework represents the remains of the castle built by Sorley Boy McDonnell, who was born in 1505 and lived to the age of 84. Dunluce was seized by Sorley Boy in 1558 after the death of his brother Colla, who had married the daughter of the McQuillan chief in 1544. Sorley Boy was evicted by Shane O'Neill in 1565 and again in 1584 by Sir John Perrott, but he managed to regain possession with the aid of artillery. He was officially appointed Constable of Dunluce by Queen Elizabeth in 1586.

Repairs to the castle were needed on the landward side, and new work included the addition of a gatehouse with turrets in the Scottish style. Cannon ports in the curtain wall were evidently added to make use of the four cannons taken from the *Girona*, a galliass from the Spanish Armada which was

Perched high on a cliff, Dunluce has always been an important defensive site. The ruins we see today date from the 14th century, but its history goes back much further.

wrecked nearby, on Lacada Point at the Giant's Causeway. A very unusual feature is the north-facing Italian-style loggia installed behind the curtain wall in the 1560s. This feature was copied from Scottish castles, but it was later blocked, in 1636, by the building of a lavish three-storey gabled house for Lady Catherine McDonnell, wife of Randal MacDonnell, the second Earl of Antrim.

Inventories show that this house had magnificent furnishings, including cast-off curtains from Cardinal Wolsey's Hampton Court Palace. Lady Catherine had big ideas – she was after all the widow of the assassinated Duke of Buckingham. She may have been responsible for the creation of the mainland court, which was built to replace the lower yard when some of its domestic buildings, including the kitchen, fell into the sea along with most of the servants in 1639.

The Earl and Countess of Antrim lived in great style, frequently attending Charles I's court in London, where they picked up most of their furnishings.

The second earl was a Royalist, and was arrested by Parliamentarian troops at Dunluce in 1642. After that the family stopped living at Dunluce Castle, which gradually slid into decay. The ruined castle remained the property of the Earls of Antrim until 1928, when it was handed over to the state for preservation.

MELLIFONT ABBEY

LOCATION **COUNTY LOUTH, EIRE**

DATE BUILT *c.* **1150**

FOUNDER **MALACHY, FORMER ARCHBISHOP OF ARMAGH**

In 1140, Malachy, the former Archbishop of Armagh, went on a pilgrimage to Rome with some disciples. On his way to and from Rome he visited Clairvaux, where he met the great St Bernard. He was so impressed that he wanted to set up a community in Ireland on the Clairvaux model.

Bernard kept four of Malachy's disciples for training, while Malachy sought a suitable place for an abbey. He eventually found an isolated spot on the River Mattock, not far from Drogheda. It was in the territory of King Donnchadh of Airghialla, who supported the religious reform movement. The king gave the land to the Cistercian Order and the first monks arrived from Clairvaux to set up the abbey. They included Robert, the abbey's architect.

In 1152, the new Mellifont Abbey hosted the Synod of Drogheda, though the abbey church was not consecrated until five years later. Mellifont grew in importance, and by the end of the 12th century it had spawned 23 daughter houses. The arrival of the Anglo-Normans in Ireland in 1169 created friction in the Irish Cistercian houses. After Abbot Thomas ordered the monastery doors closed to visitors, the rebellion spread to other Cistercian monasteries in Ireland and became known as 'the Mellifont Conspiracy'.

Mellifont Abbey declined in the 14th and 15th centuries. In 1471, the Chapter General took action against Mellifont as it was on the verge of ruin. Abbot John Troy launched a series of reforms, but his successor let things go again – and then the Reformation overtook the abbey in 1539. It is said that a small group of monks stayed on, but the Cistercians began to disperse and in 1718, the last Cistercian Abbot of Mellifont died.

In the 20th century the Cistercians founded a new monastery at Mellifont and in 1945 it became an abbey once more. Today the visible remains are not the original 12th-century buildings, though the outlines of the earlier church can be seen in the chancel and transepts, which were extended in the rebuilding. The abbey church has a unique crypt at its west end, probably designed to give the building structural support.

CLIFDEN CASTLE

LOCATION **COUNTY GALWAY, EIRE**
DATE BUILT **19TH CENTURY**
FOUNDER **JOHN D'ARCY**

Clifden Castle in Connemara is a modest castle, a miniature masterpiece in Gothic Revival style. The builder, John D'Arcy was a man of considerable determination and energy, founding Clifden town as well as the castle.

D'Arcy founded the town in 1812, and built his castle there, for his own use, at about the same time. He had 14 children by two successive wives, so the castle must have been a very full and lively family home.

John D'Arcy died in 1839, leaving both the castle and the town to his eldest son, Hyacinth D'Arcy. But these were difficult times in the West of Ireland and it was a bitter legacy that Hyacinth was left. The Great Famine of the 1840s caused misery throughout the community. The poor starved and the landowners could not expect any rent from them. The famine caused Hyacinth D'Arcy to run up huge debts and he went bankrupt. In 1850, both the town and the castle were up for sale. Hyacinth D'Arcy lost them.

The new owners of Clifden Castle were the Eyre family from Bath in England. They bought the town and castle for £21,245 and lived in the castle until the 1920s. Then the properties were bought by the state and divided up among the tenants. The castle had no outright owner and fell into neglect. It then suffered the fate of many another castle in earlier centuries, becoming a quarry for building materials and quickly became a modern ruin.

One curious feature of Clifden is the standing stones. D'Arcy had them raised to mimic the ancient megalithic monuments of Ireland. D'Arcy liked to pretend they were ancient, but they are not.

The masonry shell of the castle is in a surprisingly good state of preservation. It is possible to walk inside the house by way of an entrance through the back garden, but no longer possible to enter from the front.

At first glance, on approaching it, Clifden Castle appears intact. It is only when you notice that there is no glass in any of the windows that you realize that Clifden is derelict. It is a sad end to a fine house.

TRIM CASTLE

LOCATION **COUNTY MEATH, EIRE**

DATE BUILT **1224 (ON SITE OF EARLIER CASTLE)**

FOUNDER **DE LACY FAMILY**

Just three years after the Anglo-Normans invaded Ireland, a Norman magnate called Hugh de Lacy built a round motte (an artificial castle mound) with a timber tower on top.

This was the first fortification to be built at Trim, in 1173. It was the first step in the Anglo-Norman conquest of County Meath. Rory O'Connor, King of Connaught and last High King of Ireland, recognized the significance of the building, felt threatened by its presence and assembled an army to destroy it. The constable in charge, Hugh Tyrell, set fire to the timber castle and abandoned it before King Rory O'Connor arrived.

King John visited Trim in 1210 to hold the de Lacy family in check. His visit gave the castle its alternative name, King John's Castle, but this is misleading as Walter de Lacy locked it up and left town, leaving the king to camp in a meadow outside. King John never actually stayed at Trim Castle.

When King John encountered Trim Castle and its locked gates it had begun to take on its present appearance as the first, largest and most formidable stone castle in Ireland. Walter de Lacy started the replacement of the wooden tower with a stone castle, but this transformation was not completed until 1224. De Lacy's grandson-in-law Geoffrey de Geneville oversaw the second stage in the castle's development. Geoffrey was a crusader who later became a Dominican monk at the abbey he himself founded nearby.

Henry of Lancaster, later to become King Henry IV of England, was imprisoned in the Dublin Gate on the southern reach of the outer wall.

Trim was taken by Silken Thomas in 1536 and in 1647 by Catholic forces who opposed the English Parliamentarians. Trim was taken again by Cromwellian troops under Charles Coote in 1649, when the castle and town walls were badly damaged. The castle never recovered from this slighting.

Today the green three-acre castle enclosure is dominated by a classic Norman keep 25 metres (82 ft) high and with square corner towers, set on a motte. Inside are three storeys, the lowest divided by a central wall. The main outer wall was built in around 1250, and it is an impressive fortification in its own right, 500 metres (1,640 ft) long and still more or less intact, in spite of the Parliamentarian onslaught. This curtain wall is interrupted by eight massive round towers and a gatehouse. Within the north corner was a church. Facing the River Boyne which acts as a moat on one side was a Royal Mint, which produced 'Patricks' and 'Irelands' (Irish coins) on into the 15th century. With its Norman keep and impressive curtain wall, Trim is reminiscent of Pevensey in Sussex.

Today the green three-acre Trim Castle enclosure is dominated by a classic Norman keep with square corner towers and set on a motte.

Excavations in 1971 south of the keep uncovered the remains of ten headless men, who were probably criminals executed in the late middle ages. In 1465, Edward IV ordered that anyone who committed a robbery, or 'was going to rob', should be beheaded; their heads were mounted on spikes and publicly displayed as a warning to others.

MALAHIDE CASTLE

LOCATION **COUNTY DUBLIN, EIRE**
DATE BUILT **12TH CENTURY**
FOUNDER **TALBOT FAMILY**

Malahide means 'on the brow of the sea', and it stands on a low hill overlooking a bay north of Dublin. Its park has fine mature oaks and chestnuts dating to the 16th century.

Malahide Castle is unique in remaining the property of one family, the Talbots, for over 790 years. The Talbot family became lords of Malahide in 1185 and occupied it until 1976, apart from an interlude in the mid-17th century when Cromwell took Malahide from the Catholic Royalist Talbots. After the Restoration the family got their castle back. From the 18th century onwards it was developed as a great mansion.

The heart of the medieval castle is the oak room, which is approached by a winding stair and lit by Gothic windows added in 1820. The room is lined from floor to ceiling with carved oak panels showing scenes from scripture. It is likely that the Talbots covertly used this room as a family chapel at times when it was dangerous to be openly Catholic. Next to it is the great hall, added in 1475; unique in Ireland, this hall kept its original form and function, remaining a dining room until 1976. The huge painting of the Battle of the Boyne (1690) is a poignant reminder that on the morning of the historic battle 14 Talbot cousins, all of them followers of the Catholic James II, gathered to eat in the Great Hall at Malahide; not one returned.

The early medieval castle was enlarged and embellished in the time of Edward IV. The architect added round corner turrets to the exterior as a concession to the latest Gothic style. The facade was made incomparably grander in 1765 when two big flanking round towers were added.

When Lord Talbot de Malahide died unexpectedly in 1973, his sister inherited the property together with crippling death duties. The wonderful collection of furniture had to be sold at auction. Much was bought by the Irish Tourist Board who have reinstated it. The National Gallery purchased 35 of the family portraits and returned them on loan. As a result of these rescue measures, the interior of Malahide Castle retains much of its original character and beauty.

CORCOMROE ABBEY

LOCATION **COUNTY CLARE, EIRE**
DATE BUILT *c.* **1185**
FOUNDER **KING DONAL MOR O'BRIEN**

Corcomroe Abbey is picturesquely located in a green valley among the grey, windswept limestone hills of the Burren. The place is off the beaten track and visitors often find themselves alone in the abbey ruins.

The abbey was founded in about 1185 by King Donal Mor O'Brien as a Cistercian community. Corcomroe Abbey's nickname, Saint Mary of the Fertile Rock, tells us why the valley site was chosen; it was a place where the community could support itself by growing its own food. Set back a little from the coast, it was comparatively safe from the many pirate bands who systematically raided small coastal communities.

Most of the buildings have now gone, except the church, which is very well preserved though unroofed and a few other stretches of wall around, all built of hard grey limestone. The church is cross-shaped with a chapel leading out of each transept, though one of these is now sealed off because it contains burials. The decorated pillar capitals carry the only Irish botanical carvings to be found from the 12th century. Some more interesting carved images are to be seen in the transept chapels, which include masks with human faces and ingeniously carved dragons' heads. The choir has somehow kept its fine stone vault, which is criss-crossed by finely carved rib vaulting in Romanesque style. There is also a triple lancet window at the east end.

In the north wall of the choir there is a tomb-niche containing a remarkable effigy of King Conor na Siudaine O'Brien. This is a great rarity – one of the very few surviving images of a medieval Irish king. He wears a calf-length pleated gown and a spiked crown and carries a sceptre in his left hand.

After the Dissolution of the monasteries in 1554, the abbey was passed to the Earl of Thomond, Murrough O'Brien, and then on to Donal O'Brien, the last native prince. Strangely, it seems that monks were still formally attached to Corcomroe Abbey, as in 1628 a monk was appointed as abbot.

In the 19th century, the half-ruined church and its grounds were used as a graveyard, and the site is still a focal point for the local community.

BUNRATTY CASTLE

LOCATION COUNTY CLARE, EIRE

DATE BUILT 15TH CENTURY (ON SITE OF 1270s CASTLE)

FOUNDER MCNAMARA CLAN

Bunratty (Bun Raite) Castle overlooks the River Shannon not far from Limerick. Its strategic position at the head of the Shannon estuary made it an inevitable focus for many a bloody battle.

Its location meant that it was repeatedly destroyed and rebuilt – no less than eight times, in fact. Surprisingly, in view of this history of multiple destructions, today Bunratty Castle is in excellent condition and it is without question the finest surviving example of an Irish tower house.

Bunratty Castle had its beginnings more than a thousand years ago. In 950, the Vikings built a fortified trading post on this spot, which was once an island defended by a natural moat. When the Anglo-Normans arrived they recognized its strategic value and built the first stone structure on the site; Thomas de Clare built the first castle at Bunratty some time in the 1270s.

The very fine and impressive structure that we see today, with its high arch and two flanking square towers, dates from the 15th century, and it has walls 3 metres (10 ft) thick that soar over five storeys high. It was the McNamara clan who built Bunratty, in 1425, but they did not hold onto it for very long. Subsequently Bunratty fell into the hands of the O'Briens, the Princes of Thomond, and they held it until the 17th century.

In the walls there are three murder holes. These enabled defenders to pour boiling water onto attackers below. The castle's centrepiece is its great hall, which is decorated with collections of medieval and Renaissance paintings, furniture and wall hangings: a major tourist attraction.

The Studdart family, an Anglo-Irish family, acquired Bunratty Castle in 1720 and lived in it until the 19th century. Then they abandoned it and built Bunratty House, which stands on a hill

After 1804 Bunratty Castle was allowed to fall into disrepair when the Studdart family abandoned it and built Bunratty House. The castle was to return to its former splendour after its purchase by the state in 1954.

opposite the castle. In 1954 the castle was bought by the state and restored to its present splendid condition. The extensive restoration work was supported by the Office of Public Works, the Irish Tourist Board and Shannon Development; it is now managed by the Shannon Development Company, which organizes twice-nightly four-course medieval Bunratty banquets complete with wine, medieval menus, court jesters and Irish harpists. The company also runs the adjacent Folk Park with its reconstructed traditional Irish village where costumed characters demonstrate traditional skills. The whole complex has been deliberately developed to make it into one of Ireland's top tourist attractions.

The castle is a very simple but impressive building: it is a high and massive cube-shaped chunk of masonry resolving into big square towers at each corner, and with a battlemented roofline. In some ways it looks like a Norman keep, which historically was its point of origin; but the rather exotic battlements and the huge recessed central arch make it look more like something middle eastern, such as the Gate of Ishtar in Babylon.

Bunratty Castle is a very imposing and intriguing building and a deservedly popular tourist attraction. The most complete and authentically restored and furnished castle in Ireland, it is now open to visitors throughout the year.

CASHEL CASTLE

LOCATION COUNTY TIPPERARY, EIRE

DATE BUILT 5TH CENTURY

FOUNDER KINGS OF MUNSTER

The Rock of Cashel, or Rock of St Patrick, is a magnificent place, a great multiple ruin on a limestone hill at the edge of Cashel. Turning a bend in the main road between Dublin and Cork, the visitor is suddenly confronted by an extraordinary cluster of ancient buildings of different ages and purposes, like a miniature medieval city.

The fortress dates back to the fifth century AD and it has important links with early Christianity. This was Cashel, 'the stone fort', the seat of Irish kings and bishops through a period of 900 years. It was in its early days a royal fortress of the Eoghanacht clan, the rulers of the old Irish kingdom of Munster, for 400 years; their stronghold at Cashel witnessed the violent struggle by the Kings of Munster for power over the whole of Ireland.

In the 970s, the O'Neills of the north of Ireland were the dominant Irish clan. Things changed when Brian Boru was crowned King of Munster at Cashel in 977. He was probably crowned on the plinth of an ancient cross, the traditional crowning place of the Kings of Munster. Boru was a great warrior, and his prowess was such that in 997 the King of the O'Neills agreed on a division of Ireland with him. Brian Boru was not satisfied with half of Ireland and, when Dublin and Leinster revolted in 999, Boru put down their rebellion with such violence that the King of the O'Neills submitted to him in 1002.

In this way Brian Boru, working from his fortress at Cashel, succeeded in making himself High King of Ireland. During the next four years, Brian Boru undertook two tours of Ireland to show himself as high king of the whole island of Ireland. This

The striking round tower was added when the fortified site was taken over by the church and a cathedral built within the fortress walls.

technique of peregrination was very important, then and in later centuries; people needed to see their monarch, even if only occasionally, in order to feel any loyalty to him.

But Brian Boru's glory was shortlived. Leinster and Dublin rebelled again in 1013, provoking Boru to attack Leinster and lay siege to Dublin. He made the mistake of going home to celebrate Christmas. When he returned in 1014, the Vikings in Dublin had summoned extra troops from Scotland. The major battle that followed was the Battle of Clontarf, in which thousands died. Boru's army won, but Brian Boru himself was killed.

After that the O'Neill clan regained their dominant position. From having been the seat of the High King of Ireland, Cashel and Munster dwindled in significance. In the 12th century, the high king at that time, Rory O'Connor of Connaught, conquered Munster before going on to attack Dublin.

Interwoven with this struggle for political power is another story, the ecclesiastical history of Cashel. Aenghus, King of Munster in the fifth century, was converted to Christianity by St Patrick. Following this conversion Patrick created a bishopric at Cashel. In 1101, the Rock of Cashel was granted to the church and Bishop Cormac MacCarthy began work building a chapel. It still survives and is the most remarkable Romanesque church in the whole of Ireland. An impressive round tower was added. Perhaps the most imposing building on the rock is the 13th-century cathedral.

Altogether, the Rock of Cashel complex amounts to the most impressive collection of medieval buildings to be found anywhere in Ireland.

ROSS CASTLE

LOCATION COUNTY KERRY, EIRE

DATE BUILT 15TH CENTURY

FOUNDER O'DONAGHUE CLAN

Ross Castle, which stands proudly on the shore of Killarney's Lower Lake, is one of the finest surviving examples of a medieval Irish chieftain's stronghold.

The visible castle is thought to have been built in the middle of the 15th century by the O'Donaghue clan, though this structure may well replace an earlier stronghold. Its most conspicuous feature is a tall and graceful stone tower or keep, a fine building in itself, with its corner tower and battlements. It was fitted with square bartizans, or corner turrets, which were built out from the upper walls at battlement level at opposite corners of the keep. The turrets enabled occupants to drop missiles on attackers below, but, perhaps more importantly, gave them a full view of the exterior of each wall.

The castle's great square tower stands in a square enclosure or bawn, which is surrounded by a fine battlemented curtain wall with round corner towers. Two of these towers are still standing. The other two were demolished in 1688 to make room for an extension, and the ruins of this can be seen on the south side of the castle.

Ross Castle was the seat and main stronghold of the O'Donaghue Mors, who were the hereditary rulers of the Killarney district; they were also the descendants of the ancient kings of Munster. After the Desmond rebellion their lands were acquired by the MacCarthy Mors, who sold them on to Sir Valentine Browne, the ancestor of the Earls of Kenmare.

In 1652, Ross Castle was held by Lord Muskerry against a besieging Cromwellian army; it finally fell to the Parliamentarian forces after floating batteries were brought in across the lough to bombard it. In 1690, the castle's owners were still the Browne family. They had their property confiscated for supporting the Jacobite cause, not regaining their lands until 1720.

The Brownes built themselves a new house a little to the north of the castle, and closer to the town. In time, as the military usefulness of the castle declined and it was abandoned, the castle turned into a kind of folly, in effect a very large-scale garden feature. Ross Castle Lodge now functions as a hotel.

BLARNEY CASTLE

LOCATION **COUNTY CORK, EIRE**

DATE BUILT **15TH CENTURY (ON SITE OF EARLIER CASTLE)**

FOUNDER **MCCARTHY FAMILY**

Blarney Castle stands, with its village beside it, just 5 miles (8 km) to the north-west of Cork. It was created on the site of what was once a hunting lodge in the tenth century.

Blarney is one of those castle names that have strong resonances and associations that go beyond architecture, history or archaeology. Like Balmoral, Harlech and Caernarvon, the name has a strong, characterful acquired meaning that goes far beyond the geography and history of the place. 'Blarney' means something special – even to those who have never been there. Above all, it is thoroughly Irish.

The castle was originally a timber hunting lodge for the local chiefs, and a thousand years on it still stands in wooded country that has changed but little in all that time. The hunting lodge was rebuilt as a strong stone castle in 1210. The building that we see at Blarney today represents a third structure on the same site, a 15th-century castle that was completed by the local chief, Dermot McCarthy, in 1446.

The castle remained the ancestral stronghold of the McCarthy family for exactly 200 years, withstanding several sieges until Oliver Cromwell and his cannon arrived to lay siege to it in 1646. Then the McCarthys were thrown out. Fifteen years later, after the restoration of Charles II, the McCarthys were given their castle back and they took up residence there again.

After the Battle of the Boyne in 1690, all of the Irish chieftains were stripped of their powers, and many were evicted from their strongholds. The McCarthys were once more forced out of their castle, having regained it only a generation earlier. Blarney Castle was then largely demolished to make it indefensible before it was sold to Sir James Jeffryes, the Governor of Cork, in 1703.

The keep at Blarney Castle is a very powerful and impressive square building soaring 26 metres (85 ft) into the air on stout walls 4 metres (13 ft) thick. It looks even taller than this because it is perched picturesquely on a cliff edge. The massive keep is built five storeys high on an L-shaped plan.

Blarney Castle is one of Ireland's oldest and most historic castles and is the third structure to be built on this site. It is, of course, known for its famous Blarney Stone.

The lowest two levels are covered by a pointed stone vault. The slender tower that contains the main staircase and a few small chambers is evidently older than the main block. The keep is crowned with high, stepped battlements that jut out a full 60 cm (24 in) from the wall top; the overhang is supported by long inverted pyramid-shaped corbels, giving the castle a distinctive look and texture. This is crenellation on the grand scale, and it turns the keep into a very fine building.

The castle is best known for its Blarney Stone. This is a block of limestone a metre long, mounted high up on the wall of the keep, just below the battlements on the south side. To reach it, one has to climb one of the stone spiral staircases to the battlements. The stone is said to be one half of the Stone of Scone. This stone famously sat under the Coronation Chair in Westminster Abbey for several centuries, and has only recently been returned to Scotland, from where it was stolen by the English in the middle ages.

The Stone of Scone was an ancient crowning stone, rather like the 'King's Stone' at Kingston-on-Thames. The Blarney Stone is said to have been given to Cormac McCarthy by King Robert the Bruce in 1314 in recognition of his support at the Battle of Bannockburn. On the other hand, the Stone of Scone originated in Ireland and was taken to Scotland in the dark ages, so it may after all be that the Blarney Stone represents a portion of the crowning stone that never left Ireland.

Probably it was a common practice in the dark ages for kings throughout the so-called Celtic lands to be installed while sitting or standing on a specially sanctified stone. At Tintagel Castle in Cornwall there is a carved footprint, which was probably used by Dumnonian kings

during their dark age 'crowning' ceremonies. We may never know where the Blarney Stone came from, or why it was considered so special.

The strange connection between the stone and 'blarney' is explained by an episode in the 16th century. Elizabeth I wanted the chiefs of Ireland to agree to occupy their lands under title from her; she wanted them to acknowledge her overlordship. The Lord of Blarney, Cormac Teige McCarthy, was repeatedly asked for his submission to Elizabeth by George Cardew, who was Elizabeth's Deputy in Ireland. Cormac handled each and every one of these requests with tact and subtle diplomacy, fulsomely promising his loyalty to the queen, though carefully without conceding the issue of overlordship. Cardew duly reported this back to the queen, who exploded, 'Blarney! What he says he never means. It's the usual Blarney!' After that the word Blarney became proverbial for 'the gift of the gab', empty promises or placation with smooth-talking deception; we still use it today, more than 400 years later.

Kissing the Blarney Stone is a slightly risky business, but it is said that those who risk it magically acquire Cormac Teige McCarthy's honey tongue. It's still a popular activity, however, so the stone is disinfected four times a day.

Today Blarney Castle forms part of an estate offering some pleasant woodland walks, the Blarney Castle Estate. Just 200 metres (656 ft) south of the castle stands Blarney House, which was built in 1874. In the 18th century Sir John Jefferys built a Gothic-Revival-style house onto the castle, adding pointed windows and fanciful curving pinnacled battlements to his creation. Sad to say, this very picturesque house was burnt down in about 1820; only a semi-circular staircase from it still remains.

Close by, the family built themselves a Scottish-Baronial-style house overlooking the lake – and, for good measure, added a megalithic garden folly. Clearly the tradition of good-natured eccentricity, the true spirit of Ireland, has been thoroughly maintained at Blarney Castle.

TIMOLEAGUE ABBEY

LOCATION **COUNTY CORK, EIRE**

DATE BUILT **1240**

FOUNDER **MACCARTHY REACH**

Timoleague Abbey stands on the edge of Timoleague village, which today is a colourful and prosperous little community just a few steps from a sea inlet opening onto the Atlantic.

The abbey had the benefit of being able to trade by sea, from which it gained some profit, though there were always risks in being a coastal community. It was built on the site of St Molga's Well. Like many other wells, this was probably a pagan cult focus before it was adopted and converted by Christians. Around 1200 of these holy wells are known to have existed, and certainly many more have been lost. One of the finest Christian chapels to be built over a converted sacred spring is at Holywell in Clwyd. Probably the well at Timoleague was of the same type, only it had an abbey built over it.

Timoleague Abbey was founded in 1240 by MacCarthy Reach, Lord Carbery, and extended in 1312 by Donal Glas McCarthy. The buildings on the site date from various periods, and the abbey was extended again in the early 16th century, by Irish patrons, shortly before the Dissolution. Certainly the current church, a roofless ruin but with its tower intact, is not the first to stand on the site. The original church was shorter. It was probably lengthened when the portion including the tower was added by Edmund de Courcy, Bishop of Ross, late in the 15th century.

In 1642, Timoleague Abbey was sacked by English soldiers who burnt it down. Even so, a lot of the original stonework has survived. The church, the infirmary, the refectory and a walled courtyard are all still standing. There are also cloisters and a wine cellar. The architecture of Timoleague was very plain and must have been very austere even when complete. But the friars who lived there did not live austere lives. They had a penchant for the finer things in life, and were prosperous thanks to their trade with Spanish wine merchants.

As at other religious houses in Ireland, Timoleague survived the Reformation, for a time. The friars were able to remain at the abbey until 1629. Today, Timoleague Abbey is a rather sad-looking roofless ruin, but it still acts as a graveyard for the local people.

WALES

BEAUMARIS CASTLE

LOCATION **ISLE OF ANGLESEY, WALES**

DATE BUILT **1295–1330**

FOUNDER **KING EDWARD I**

It was in 1295 that building work started on this castle. The building began immediately after the Welsh rising under Madog ap Llewellyn had been suppressed, but lack of funds meant that it was never completed.

'Beau Mareys' is a Norman French phrase meaning 'fair marsh'. Marshes were often shunned for settlement because they were damp and seen as a source of ague (malaria), but they were ideal for defence. Attackers could march or ride across dry land, or use boats across water, but there was no quick or efficient way of getting heavily armed men across a marsh.

Beaumaris Castle came late in the sequence of great castles of oppression built on the orders of Edward I, at a time when money was short, yet it was still designed by Edward's chief military architect, Master James of St George. After designing the earlier castles, Beaumaris was set to be his masterpiece.

At the peak of the building project, Beaumaris employed 2600 men. But by 1298 the funds required for completion had run out and the work had to stop. Building began again between 1306 and 1330, but with both the workforce and the design at a reduced scale. Edward I was dead and his lavish scheme was never to be completed. The accommodation planned for the gatehouse on the north side was never finished and it remained single-storey. Turrets had been planned for the round corner towers. The domestic range, with the hall, kitchens and stables, was never built.

The castle has a symmetrical and concentric layout. A very wide moat surrounds the large square curtain wall which rises straight out of the water. The outer curtain wall was relatively low. The inner defences were higher and more massive, so that defenders could fire out over the heads of those manning the outer walls. At the southern end of the moat there was a tidal dock for shipping, protected by the shooting deck on Gunners' Walk.

Beaumaris Castle is a strange and beautiful building, frozen at the time of its non-completion. It was wonderfully designed and it would have been virtually impregnable, but it was never put to the test.

CONWY CASTLE

LOCATION **CONWY, WALES**

DATE BUILT **1283-7**

FOUNDER **KING EDWARD I**

Conwy Castle is by any standards one of the great fortresses of medieval Europe. Along with Harlech and Caernarfon, Conwy ranks among the most impressive of all the castles in Wales.

All three castles were designed by Master James of St George. Conwy differs from Harlech in having a well-preserved town wall. A similar town wall was built at Caernarfon but it is far less complete and is rather lost amid the later developments of the modern town. Conwy's wall gives its town a very distinctive, indeed unique, medieval flavour that other Welsh castle towns have lost.

Work began on the construction of Conwy Castle in 1283, when it was conceived as an important link in Edward I's strategy to surround Wales with an iron ring of castles. As at Caernarfon, Edward I set up a colony settlement at Conwy, and the town wall was necessary to defend the incoming English settlers from the native Welsh population, who naturally opposed the colonization violently. In the town square at Conwy stands a poignant statue of Llewellyn the Great, the heroic Welsh leader and founder of Welsh Conwy who died in 1240, 40 years before the English king arrived to take it over.

It was during Edward I's second campaign in Wales that he gained control of the Conwy valley, in March 1283. Work began on the new fortress immediately, and Master James, who was Master of the King's Works in Wales, must have worked very fast indeed to produce the design for the building work to have started so quickly. A much older fortress stood on the hill on the opposite side of the Conwy estuary, Castell Degannwy. This was a fortress in the Iron Age and was later reoccupied and refortified as the stronghold of King Maelgwn in the middle of the sixth century; it continued to be used through the middle ages until the castle was built at Conwy. The site chosen by Edward I in discussion with Master James was a better defensive site, and the low-altitude location was more suitable for the garrison-town that was to stand beside the new castle, all to be surrounded by a town wall.

Conwy Castle and the town wall were built in a frenzy of activity in just four years, between 1283 and 1287, involving 1500 craftsmen and labourers. Master James may have abandoned the very successful concentric design because of the restricted nature of the site, as at Caernarfon. The texture of the rock outcrop chosen for the site dictated a linear shape, with a barbican at each end. Again as at Caernarfon, the enclosure was divided in two by a cross-wall to create two separate wards. This was a precaution against the breaching of the curtain wall; if either ward should be penetrated by attackers, the other could be held as an independent stronghold.

When they were finished, the masonry walls were covered with a plastered and whitewashed rendering. This would have made the castle dazzlingly conspicuous in the landscape, adding a further layer of intimidation to the rebellious Welsh. It would also have had the practical value of concealing the joints and courses in the masonry, along with any other weak points that the attackers might exploit. Some fragments of this medieval rendering can still be seen on the walls.

Most visitors approach Conwy from the east and the castle seems to jump up suddenly out of the hills. The much later, but still majestic, suspension bridge that connects the castle with the

With its massive curtain wall and strong towers, Conwy Castle still appears impenetrable, even today.

main peninsula guards the principal entrance to the castle. The castle dominates the approach to Conwy, conveying an impression of great strength and compactness. Like Caernarfon, Conwy consists of a single large-walled enclosure, by contrast to the concentric design seen at Beaumaris. The huge curtain wall surrounding the castle connects eight huge towers, all still intact. The design forms a rectangle, an unusually regular plan for an Edwardian castle.

Conwy Castle has a very unified and strong design. Its towers are almost identical, four on the north, four on the south, nailing the castle to the living rock. The north front is particularly striking. The towers

are evenly spaced, dividing the curtain wall into three exactly similar segments, each pierced with a pair of arrow loops and all rising to the same battlement line. It is still possible to tour the wall-walks and climb from them to the tops of the towers; from these vantage points it is easy to appreciate the castle's layout.

The inner ward contains the suite Master James built for King Edward and Queen Eleanor in 1283. In each range the main rooms were on the first floor above dark basements. Unfortunately all the floors have now gone.

The town wall is remarkably well preserved, surviving round almost the entire circuit of the town. Only one short section is inaccessible, near the quay, and even there it still exists, incorporated into later buildings. A spur wall projecting 60 metres (197 ft) from the end of the quay gives excellent views of the castle. It is 1,400 metres (4,593 ft) long and links together 21 towers and three twin-towered gateways. As at Caernarfon, the town wall should be regarded as part of Master James's integral design; in spite of appearances, Conwy is functionally concentric.

Edward I was besieged at Conwy during Madog ap Llewellyn's rebellion in 1295. The walls stood firm, proving the high quality of Master James's design and workmanship, though food supplies ran low. Eventually, in 1403, Conwy Castle was taken, though by trickery rather than any weakness in the castle's architecture, and it fell to the army of the Welsh leader Owain Glendower. He later sold the castle back to the English because he was running low on funds; it would have been better if he had held onto it. After the Civil War, like many other castles, Conwy was left to the elements.

PENRHYN CASTLE

LOCATION GWYNEDD, WALES

DATE BUILT 19TH CENTURY (ON SITE OF MEDIEVAL MANSION)

FOUNDER GEORGE HAY DAWKINS-PENNANT

Penrhyn Castle, not far from Bangor, was built in the 19th century for George Hay Dawkins-Pennant, the Welsh quarry owner who had made millions out of slate.

This was an age when new men became fantastically rich on the back of the Industrial Revolution, and these new men wanted new houses with which to make their mark. Yet this was not the first great house to stand on the site. Long before, in the 14th century, Penrhyn had been the original home of the Tudor dynasty. The genuinely medieval mansion owned by the Tudors was reconstructed as a fake-medieval house in 1782 by Samuel Wyatt.

Sir Walter Scott's Romantic medieval novel *Ivanhoe* was published in 1820 and sparked a Norman revival. Thomas Hopper was commissioned by George Hay Dawkins-Pennant to do a Norman make-over of Penrhyn Castle. Hopper was a very versatile architect, working on the principle that 'it is an architect's business to understand all styles and be prejudiced in favour of none'. It was a principle he lived by, too.

For his Normanized Penrhyn Castle, Hopper imported quantities of hard grey Mona marble from Anglesey, and he conscientiously kept to a Norman decorative scheme throughout. The keep is colossal, 35 metres (115 ft) high and 19 metres (62 ft) wide, a big sombre building that Hopper modelled on the keep at Rochester Castle in Kent. Rather oddly, the monumental keep does not stand in the middle of the complex, surrounded by baileys and curtain walls, but on its own at one end of the range of buildings. There is a round ice tower, a barbican and walls that might if necessary be defended. Hopper even designed the library and drawing room in Norman style.

He made use of the material on which the family fortune was founded, slate, in a very unusual way. He had a mock Jacobean four-poster bed carved out of a four-tonne block of slate, as a tribute to the source of Mr Dawkins-Pennant's wealth, but even that caprice had to have Norman mouldings.

The end result of Thomas Hopper's endeavour was a great showpiece, an extravaganza, and a stunning tribute to the power of Scott's novel.

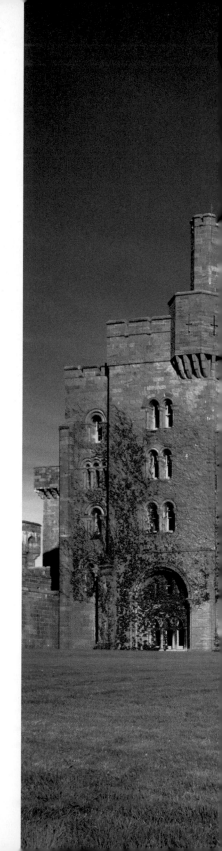

CAERNARFON CASTLE

LOCATION **GWYNEDD, WALES**
DATE BUILT **1283–85**
FOUNDER **KING EDWARD I**

Caernarfon is Wales's Windsor, standing as a mighty symbol of the greatness of the English monarchs. As such, this castle holds the history of Wales in a steely grip. It was begun in 1283 at the orders of Edward I, to be one of a chain of castles to subdue and control the Welsh.

Caernarfon stands at the south-western end of the Menai Strait, the sleeve of water separating Anglesey from the mainland of North Wales. It was an excellent choice of location. Anglesey was the garden of Wales, providing agriculturally rich land and therefore a reliable food supply, close to the otherwise poor land of North Wales. The Menai Strait also allowed swift access by sea to the coasts of North Wales and West Wales; from there it was possible for Edward I's forces to move quickly to Conwy or Harlech. Like all the other castles in Edward's iron ring, Caernarfon was built on the shoreline, to ensure the safe delivery of supplies. Although there were roads across Wales, the Welsh were good at ambush and other forms of guerrilla warfare. Locating castles by the sea, the English could be fairly sure they would not be cut off.

Caernarfon had its origins in a Roman fort, Segontium, which was set up on a low hill to the south-east of the present town. After the Romans withdrew from Britain, in 380–90, the fort was occupied by local chieftains. Later the district round it became one of the 'manors' of the princes of Gwynedd. In the dark ages it was Conwy that emerged as the seat of the kings of Gwynedd, but Edward I selected Caernarfon as the capital of the principality of North Wales. This marked it out as a key political and military centre, and it explains why Edward wanted Caernarfon Castle to be special.

Before Edward I's masterpiece was built, a Norman motte and bailey castle had stood on the site. It was raised around the year 1090. This motte was incorporated into the later medieval fortress, but was unfortunately destroyed in 1870. The Welsh recaptured the original motte in 1115 and kept it until Edward I's invasion and colonization of 1283. The work at

Caernarfon began in May 1283, after Edward's march into North Wales from Chester. The king's intention was to create a nucleus of English influence in this area, which was one rich in Welsh tradition and anti-English feeling. Caernarfon was to be a colony settlement.

Edward I is known for the building of Caernarfon Castle. What is less often remembered is that he destroyed the Welsh town that stood beside it and replaced it with an English town. This was ruthless conquest with a vengeance.

Materials for building the castle and town were brought in by sea. The first recorded entry of the project, on 24 June 1283, was the digging of the castle's new ditch. The next step was to raise a wooden palisade to protect the building work from attack. The main priority in the first building phase was to make the site defensible. The walls of the castle and the town were more or less completed by the end of 1285. The remarkably gifted architect of this first phase was Edward I's chief castle builder, Master James of St George.

By the end of the first building phase, the north side of the castle still had no wall; it was instead defended by the town wall and a rock-cut ditch. Madog ap Llewellyn used this weak point to attack the castle in his rebellion of 1294. The English had little difficulty in retaking Caernarfon Castle the following summer and it was made defensible again; repairs were made and the north curtain wall of the castle was finally built, including the King's Gate.

The great castle was not completed until the reign of Edward II, in 1322, by which time it looked much as it does today, the conception of a single military mind – Master James of St George. It had cost £25,000 to build and was easily the grandest, noblest castle Edward I had built. The Welsh hated Caernarvon Castle and the English oppression that it symbolized.

Other great castles of the iron ring, Harlech and Beaumaris, were concentric, consisting of two rings of defensive walls, one within the other. Caernarfon consisted of but one curtain wall, but in a sense it was concentric – the outer wall was the town wall. Caernarfon was not just for show; Master James ensured that it was as impregnable as his other castles.

The castle had two gateways. It also had seven towers punctuating its curtain wall. The king's gate in the north wall was never completely finished, but it was still immensely strong. It was twin-towered, and was originally intended to have a drawbridge, five doors, an incredible six portcullises, to say nothing of murder holes, spy holes and arrow loops. The queen's gate was only slightly less formidably defended. The final, and major, segment of Caernarfon's defences was the wall of the town itself. This was a circuit 800 metres (2,625 ft) long with eight towers and just two twin-towered gateways. The town walls were entirely surrounded by water-filled moats, rivers and the Menai Strait.

Originally a wall across the centre of the enclosed area divided it into two wards. Once there were interior residential buildings, arranged round the curtain wall, but these were later destroyed. In spite of these losses, Caernarfon Castle is still among the best preserved castles in the British Isles.

The towers provided accommodation on several storeys. Two halls were built, the great hall and a further hall in the king's tower. The castle was designed to be able to accommodate the king's eldest son and all his household. It was Edward I's brilliant idea to create his own son 'Prince of Wales', as if conferring a great favour on the Welsh, while in fact pulling the rug from under the feet of the native princes.

All of this was designed to turn Caernarfon into the capital of a new dominion. We compared

Material for the building of the castle, town, walls, gates and important quay were ferried in by sea. All of the initial building took place as a single operation, started in the summer of 1283. The first recorded entry of work was on the new castle's ditch, separating the castle from the fortified town.

Caernarfon with Windsor, and Caernarfon was certainly planned as the seat of a great dynasty, the line of the new Prince of Wales. It was to be a stronghold, a royal palace, and a symbol of English dominion over Wales.

Edward I was conscious of what this most spectacular of all castles would look like. The walls were given a prominent patterning with bands of different coloured stone. The towers were given angular rather than circular ground plans. Edward I was making yet another powerful symbolic statement. The 13th-century walls of Caernarfon Castle bear a striking resemblance to the fifth-century walls of Constantinople. Those who had seen Constantinople would have known that Edward I was making a bold statement at Caernarfon; this castle and this city were the heart of a powerful empire.

HARLECH CASTLE

LOCATION **GWYNEDD, WALES**
DATE BUILT **1283–9**
FOUNDER **KING EDWARD I**

In Welsh mythology, Harlech is linked with the tragic heroine Branwen, daughter of Lyr. The real Harlech, the Harlech of solid grey stone, is the epitome of the medieval fortress, foursquare, with a massive round tower at each corner, and steep craggy slopes falling away on three sides.

Originally, the steep slope to the west dropped straight down to the sea, though now the accumulating sands of Morfa Harlech have left both castle and crag far from the sea, stranded and land-locked. Yet Harlech is still commanding; no castle in Britain has a finer site.

Harlech has clean and simple lines that are at the same time majestic and impregnable. It must have been even more striking when newly built in the reign of Edward I, with two high curtain walls, dazzlingly whitewashed. The castle was designed and created by Master James of St George, a military architect of pure genius. It was Master James who designed Beaumaris too. He adapted the Harlech site to make it into a perfect fortress, as part of King Edward's campaign to gain control over Snowdonia by throwing round it an iron ring of castles. These castles eventually stretched from Flint in the north-east, right round the coast to Aberystwyth in the south-west. This ambitious castle-building project was intended to prevent the region from ever becoming a focus for rebellion again.

After the Welsh stronghold of Castell y Bere fell, King Edward's army arrived at Harlech in April 1283, and Master James started building almost immediately, with a pioneer troupe of 20 quarrymen and masons. Over a six-year period, Master James organized an ever-larger team of workers until there was an army of 950 quarrymen, labourers, masons and carpenters working on the site, building Harlech Castle at high speed. Unusually, this castle was built all in one go, to a single unified design. The design was concentric, with one curtain wall

set within the other. Unfortunately the outer wall is now badly ruined and so no longer conveys the full effect of Master James's 13th-century plan.

The site chosen for the castle was perfectly defended by natural cliffs on three sides, with a rocky precipice falling to the sea on the west side. It was only the east face that was open to any possible attack from the Welsh. On this side, the gatehouse juts forbiddingly forward, defying attack from the town. The townspeople must have wondered what was happening to them as this monster was born on their doorstep.

Inside the gatehouse, the gate-passage was defended by a succession of seven obstacles, including no less than three portcullises. Guardrooms flanked the passage. On the upper floors there was accommodation for the constable or governor. From

1290–3 that constable was none other than Master James. Probably the rooms on the top floor of the gatehouse were for distinguished visitors, including the king himself.

Inside the castle's inner curtain wall, there is a surprisingly small and cramped inner ward. A lot of this space would have been taken up with domestic buildings – a chapel and bakehouse against the north wall, a granary against the south wall. There were also a great hall and kitchens; all of these domestic buildings have crumbled away through long neglect. The overall effect when all these buildings were standing must have been very cramped and claustrophobic, with the curtain wall and its towers rising 20 or more metres (65 ft) above them on all sides. The four corner towers provided more accommodation.

Even after seven centuries, Harlech Castle
remains a testament to the architect, Master
James of St George. He adapted the natural
strength of the site to the defensive requirements
of the age and created a building that combines a
marvellous sense of majesty with great beauty in
its structure and form.

There is a very fine wall-walk round the battlements of the castle, giving marvellous views in all directions. An unusual feature of Harlech Castle is the 'Way from the Sea'. This is a gated and fortified staircase that plunges from the castle 60 metres (197 ft) down to the foot of the crag. Originally, this led to the sea, which washed the foot of the rock, and enabled stores to be carried safely up to the castle from ships, but the build-up of sand has left both stairway and castle stranded. During the rising of Madog ap Lewellyn in 1294–5, this fortified stairway saved the garrison, which was victualled by ships from Ireland. The castle was so well designed that it was possible for only 37 men to defend it.

Harlech played a major role in the Welsh rising led by Owain Glendower. Glendower laid siege to Harlech, which finally fell to him in 1404, though only

through treachery, when the French fleet cut off the supply route by sea. After that, Glendower decided to make Harlech his own residence and headquarters. It is one of the places to which he summoned parliaments of his supporters. After a further siege, a reverse siege of the Welsh by the English this time, Harlech Castle was retaken by the English army in 1408. The English army was led by John Talbot, Earl of Shrewsbury. It is said that Owain Glendower had himself crowned Prince of Wales in Harlech Castle.

Later in the 15th century, during the Wars of the Roses, Harlech Castle was held by a Welsh chieftain called Dafydd ap Jevon ap Einion for the Lancastrians for a time, then taken by Sir Richard Herbert of Raglan for the Yorkists after a long siege. It was the endurance of this long siege that was the inspiration for the song *Men of Harlech*. Dafydd held out for seven years until famine forced him to give in. A chronicler wrote, 'Kyng Edward was possessed of alle Englonde, excepte a castelle in Northe Wales called Harleke.'

In the Civil War, even though the castle had fallen into 'great decaye', it held out once again in a long siege in support of Charles I, before submitting to the Parliamentarian army of General Mytton. It was the last castle to fall, which bears remarkable testimony to the wonderful engineering of Master James, the great French 'ingeniator'. It is incredible that a 13th-century castle could withstand the weaponry of the 17th century, after more than 300 years of development in military technology.

VALLE CRUCIS ABBEY

LOCATION **DENBIGHSHIRE, WALES**

DATE BUILT **EARLY 13TH CENTURY**

FOUNDER **MADOC AP GRUFFYDD MAELOR**

An isolated column known as Eliseg's Pillar stands beside to the road to Ruthin above Llangollen. It was a monument to a dark age prince of Powis, and gave its name to the valley – and to the abbey built in it – Valle Crucis, the Valley of the Cross.

The abbey was founded by Madoc ap Gruffydd Maelor, the Lord of Castell Dinas Bran, which stands on the heights above Llangollen. He had spent his life fighting and plundering. By 1201, he had decided to spend some of his wealth founding an abbey, where he himself would eventually be buried. He traced his descent from the prince of Powis commemorated by Eliseg's Pillar.

The abbey was to be built in the bottom of a deep and steep-sided valley, beside a tributary of the River Dee. The building was very plain and austere, with no ornaments other than carved capitals.

The founder's son, Gryffydd ap Madoc Maelor, married an English woman, Emma the daughter of Lord Audley. Gryffydd sided with Henry III in his campaign to subjugate the Welsh. As a result of this treachery, Gryffydd had to retreat to his hill-top fortress; when he died, he too was buried in the abbey, which by that time had been damaged in a disastrous fire.

The rebuilding was done in ashlar and the west wall of the nave is complete, with a fine door and great triple window over it and a pretty rose window like a cartwheel above that. The chapter house was rebuilt, with vaulted aisles and Decorated windows, and this has remained more or less intact, one of the best-preserved Cistercian chapter houses in Britain.

After the Dissolution Valle Crucis Abbey was granted to Sir William Pickering, who made a house out of the east range. When George Borrow visited he was unimpressed by the roofless church.

In its heyday, Valle Crucis had much to offer. Meat and wine were served to visitors and the abbot wore rings on his fingers. It was a lifestyle that was a long way from the ascetic rule of the early Cistercians – and it gave Henry VIII the excuse he wanted to close down all the abbeys.

CHIRK CASTLE

LOCATION **WREXHAM, WALES**

DATE BUILT **LATE 13TH CENTURY**

FOUNDER **ROGER MORTIMER FOR KING EDWARD I**

Chirk Castle is a 700-year-old marcher fortress, commanding fine views over the surrounding countryside. It was built in the 13th century and granted to Roger Mortimer, who was Edward I's Justice of North Wales.

The great campaign by Edward I to subdue Wales hinged on local control from castles. In Edward's ambitious scheme there were four groups of castles. There were the existing royal border castles, like Chester; there were captured native Welsh castles, like Criccieth; and there were the ten spectacular and very expensive new royal castles, such as Caernarfon. The fourth group was the new 'Lordship' castles to hold the Welsh border country and there were just four of these: Denbigh, Hawarden, Holt and Chirk. These were in law to be held in private hands, but they were built to royal architectural specifications and the building work was subsidized by the Crown.

The castle has an unusual profile, a relatively low, two-storey building with smooth battlements. The round towers and bastions are broad and squat and do not rise above the general roofline. Chirk was held for Charles I by the former Parliamentary commander Sir Thomas Myddelton in the Civil War. Once taken it proved exceptionally difficult for the Parliamentarians to slight it; General Lambert had to use enormous amounts of gunpowder to bring down one curtain wall complete with towers.

Chirk Castle was afterwards restored and is once again intact, though as a mansion with a rectangular plan including four impressive drum-shaped towers. The magnificent iron gates at the castle entrance were made in 1718. The coat-of-arms of the Myddelton family is the focal feature of the overthrow of the gates. It features the red bloody hand of the Myddeltons, three wolves' heads and an eagle's head. There are various legends to explain the red hand. One story tells of one of the early Myddeltons who badly injured his hand during a battle and clasped it to his white surcoat to staunch the bleeding. Later, he found he had left the imprint of the bloody hand on his surcoat. It was like a heraldic device, so he adopted it as one.

ABERYSTWYTH CASTLE

LOCATION **CEREDIGION, WALES**

DATE BUILT **13TH CENTURY**

FOUNDER **KING EDWARD I**

The strategic value of Aberystwyth has been recognized since the Iron Age when this site, Pen Dinas, was one of the largest hillforts in the region.

With the Norman advance into Wales came the age of the stone castle. The first castle at Aberystwyth was nevertheless an earthen ringwork castle, built by Gilbert de Clare. Later, the Welsh, led by Llewellyn the Great, built a new castle, in a high, commanding, coastal location.

In the mid-13th century Henry III tried to appease the Welsh by naming Llewellyn ap Gruffydd as Prince of Wales, but on the accession of Edward I, Llewellyn refused to pay homage to the new English king. In 1276 Edward organized his first campaign against the Welsh. The following year, he ordered the construction of a series of strongholds in Wales, as points from which English control could be maintained. They included Rhuddlan and Aberystwyth, which were designed as concentric fortresses. In its day Aberystwyth Castle was as powerful as Conwy or Harlech.

This Edwardian castle once ranked among the greatest in Wales; now it is a forlorn ruin. Its deterioration started in the 14th century. By 1343, when the Black Prince was in charge, several parts of the castle were already falling down, including the hall, the kitchen range and the main gateway. The location so close to the open sea explains the rapidity of the disintegration.

Owen Glendower seized the castle in 1404, then the English seized it back. But after 1408 Aberystwyth lost its strategic value to the English kings and they stopped spending money on repairs. In 1649, the castle fell victim to Cromwell's policy of slighting castles whose garrisons had sided with the king. After that, the castle became little more than a stone quarry for local builders.

There are, even so, enough elements surviving for the original design to be read. When complete, the diamond-shaped plan included two twin-towered gatehouses, a barbican gate and four gateways.

CILGERRAN CASTLE

LOCATION **PEMBROKESHIRE, WALES**

DATE BUILT **11TH–12TH CENTURIES**

FOUNDER **GERALD DE WINDSOR OR ROGER DE MONTGOMERY**

Cilgerran Castle has one of the finest situations of all the castles in south-west Wales. It stands on the south bank of the River Teifi and is defended on two sides by steep cliffs.

When the castle was built is disputed by historians. Some say it was built by Gerald de Windsor, the castellan of Pembroke Castle, between 1110 and 1115. Others say it was Roger de Montgomery, commander of the right flank of the Norman army at Hastings, who started building the castle in 1092.

Whoever was responsible, Cilgerran Castle was hated by local people. They attacked this symbol of oppression and conquest repeatedly and the Normans sustained heavy losses. In 1169, Gilbert de Clare, Earl of Pembroke, completed the building, probably adding the stone curtain wall at this time.

Shortly after this, the great Welsh leader Lord Rhys ap Gruffydd attacked and seized the castle. It became his principal stronghold, despite an attempt by the Normans to regain it. In 1172, Henry II stopped at Cilgerran en route for Ireland and was entertained at the castle by Lord Rhys. The Welsh occupation of a Norman stronghold was an anomaly that could not be allowed to continue indefinitely, though, and in 1204 William Marshall, Earl of Pembroke, marched on Cilgerran Castle with a huge army. His determined attack put the Welsh occupants to flight and he was able to hold the castle for a further ten years before Llewellyn ap Iorwerth retook it.

Thirteenth-century Cilgerran had inner and outer baileys, five gates and a gatehouse with portcullis and stout round towers. The walls were very thick and built of thin slate-like stones. Although it withstood a fierce onslaught in 1258, by 1275 the castle had become neglected.

The castle was garrisoned by Royalists in the Civil War and given a pounding by Parliamentarian guns. Several cannon balls from this episode have been found round the castle. The usual period of neglect followed. In 1938 it was given to the National Trust. It now consists of two courtyards or baileys and two towers, which were once known as the Red and White Towers. There are also remnants of curtain walls, chapel and a gatehouse.

ST DAVID'S CATHEDRAL

LOCATION **PEMBROKESHIRE, WALES**

DATE BUILT **12TH CENTURY (ON SITE OF EARLIER CHURCHES)**

FOUNDER **ST DAVID FOUNDED A MONASTIC SETTLEMENT HERE**

The cathedral city of St David's is no more than a village on a treeless, windswept plateau. It is the smallest cathedral city in Britain, yet it is extremely ancient, having been the seat of a bishop since the sixth century.

The cathedral is not just for St David's, it is for the whole of Pembrokeshire – south-west Wales is its sea-surrounded see. St David's Cathedral nestles on the sheltered floor of the deep wooded Alun valley below the 'city'.

The cathedral is imposing, but also a rather strange-looking building, with a tall and massive square tower and a low nave and chancel with almost flat roofs dating from 1530–40. The cathedral close still has its boundary wall and one of its gatehouses: originally there were four. The visitor approaches the cathedral by a flight of 39 steps, known as 'The Thirty-Nine Articles'.

The building we now see was begun in 1181, and it replaces at least three earlier churches on the same site, which is the spot where St David himself founded a monastic settlement in the sixth century, transferring his community from Whitesand Bay in 550, but nothing of this early settlement now survives. St David died in 589.

Because of its historic associations with the patron saint of Wales, St David's has long been a pilgrimage focus. In 1123, Bishop Bernard secured a 'privilege' from the pope to turn it into a centre for pilgrimage; two pilgrimages to St David's were equal to one to Rome. It was also a great centre of learning. In the ninth century, King Alfred asked for help from St David's in rebuilding the intellectual life of Wessex.

In 1171, Henry II visited St David's and the present cathedral building was begun. The 'new' tower fell down in 1220, and there was further damage in an earthquake in 1247. In 1648, the building was destroyed by Parliamentary soldiers. Then came the restorations. Nash rebuilt the west front in 1793 and Sir George Scott undertook restoration work 1862–77.

NARBERTH CASTLE

LOCATION **PEMBROKESHIRE, WALES**

DATE BUILT **14TH CENTURY**

FOUNDER **SIR ANDREW PERROTT**

This desolate place was called Narberth a thousand years ago. The original old mound, known as Sentence Castle, was raised nearly two miles to the south, where its round earthen motte can still be seen.

According to Welsh legend, Sentence Castle was an important stronghold, but its position laid it open to attack, which is probably why the Normans gave it up in the mid-13th century. Instead they built a stone castle at Narberth. Sentence Castle was attacked in 1113 and 1116, and again in 1215.

The new castle at Narberth was a small but imposing and strong castle, built on a natural mound just south of the town. It was rectangular in shape with round towers at each corner. It seems there was no keep.

There is one round tower that is in fair condition and standing up to three storeys high, but the rest of the castle is in a very bad state. Narberth Castle was rebuilt more than once. Sir Andrew Perrott built the stone castle in 1346, but ten years later Llewellyn ap Gruffydd, the last native Prince of Wales, attacked and destroyed it. In the reign of Edward III the castle was rebuilt again. Records show that in Narberth there was an 'Englishry' and a 'Welshry'; in other words two distinct communities were living in the area.

The castle passed to the crown in the reign of Edward III; Richard III sold it to Gruffydd ap Nicholas; Henry VIII granted it to Sir Rhys ap Thomas, who made great efforts to renovate and beautify it. Narberth was described in 1527 by John Leland as 'a little pretty pile of old Sir Rhys'.

In 1647 Narberth was bombarded by the Parliamentarian army, but after the Civil War it was still habitable. In 1677 a Captain Richard Castell, who set up large monthly cattle fairs and weekly markets at Narberth, was living there, though he is the last known resident. After Captain Castell's death the castle fell increasingly into ruin. An engraving of 1740 shows that walls, arched doorways and windows still survived, along with a gable end, some chimneys and a gateway. But today, Narberth Castle is a complete ruin.

CAREW CASTLE

LOCATION **PEMBROKESHIRE, WALES**
DATE BUILT **EARLY 12TH CENTURY**
FOUNDER **GERALD FITZWALTER**

In 1100 Arnulph de Montgomery, who had opposed the king, Henry I, found himself deprived of his possessions in Pembrokeshire. They included Pembroke Castle, which was given to Gerald Fitzwalter of Windsor, Arnulph's castellan.

Shortly after this event, Gerald Fitzwalter started building himself a new home at Carew. Gerald's eldest son, William, adopted the local place-name as his surname, following English usage, becoming de Carew.

In 1480, Carew Castle passed to Sir Rhys ap Thomas, the richest man in Wales. He backed the cause of Henry Richmond, which decided the outcome of the Wars of the Roses. Richmond, as Henry VII, did not forget Sir Rhys, making him a Garter Knight and in 1507, to celebrate his admission to the Garter, Sir Rhys held a five-day tournament at Carew Castle. It was the last great tournament ever to be held in Britain. The thing that was remembered about the event long afterwards was the remarkably high standard of behaviour at the tournament. Although a thousand men spent five days together, there was not one quarrel.

But the dark poison of politics worked on in the background. Sir Rhys's grandson, who inherited Carew Castle, was executed on Tower Hill for treason in 1531. Shortly after this, in the reign of Elizabeth I, Sir John Perrot gained the Lordship of Carew, but he too was sentenced to death for treason in 1591. The castle passed to Robert, Earl of Essex, and into other hands again. Carew Castle does not seem to have brought its owners much luck.

Carew started as a timber Norman motte and bailey castle. By 1200 it had been replaced in stone. The major part of the surviving castle dates from the 13th century. By 1250, it consisted of a single strong square enclosure with drum-shaped towers at its corners. The east front dates from 1270, as does the west front, which has great medieval dignity and strength; this was reconstructed in the reign of Henry VII by Sir Rhys. The most striking part of this fine ruin is the north front, with its great stone mullioned windows. The work of Sir John Perrot, this is a superb example of Elizabethan architecture.

137

PEMBROKE CASTLE

LOCATION **PEMBROKESHIRE, WALES**

DATE BUILT **1090**

FOUNDER **ARNULPH DE MONTGOMERY**

Pembroke Castle is a magnificent castle in a magnificent setting. It occupies a strong defensive position on a rocky hill, surrounded on three sides by a tidal river.

Arnulph de Montgomery, the Norman conqueror of Pembrokeshire and son of Roger de Montgomery, built his first fortress in the region at Pembroke in 1090. It was at first built of turf and timber, but effectively resisted attacks from the Welsh. Cadwgan ap Bleddyn tried to take it in 1092 but without success. This simple motte and bailey castle became the inner ward of the imposing stone castle that we now see.

When Arnulph returned to England, the stronghold was held by Gerald de Windsor, who was half-Norman, half-Saxon. Gerald was a brilliant castellan, who held Pembroke against a series of assaults by Welsh rebels by a combination of bravery, cunning and obstinacy. When Henry I was betrayed by Arnulph, he handed Pembroke Castle over to Gerald. It was probably Gerald who replaced the wooden palisade surrounding the inner ward with a stone wall. Gerald gradually turned Pembroke Castle into the first stone castle in Wales and the focal stronghold of 'Little England beyond Wales'.

When the earldom of Pembroke was created in 1138, Gilbert de Clare took the castle. It was Gilbert or his son Richard, known as Strongbow, who built the splendid circular Norman keep in the inner ward. It is 23 metres (75 ft) high and the finest drum keep in Britain. William Marshal held the earldom from 1189 to 1219. The great Norman Earls of Pembroke – the de Clares, the Marshals, the de Valences, the Hastings – were very powerful magnates, powerful enough to risk defying the kings of England several times. One of the most powerful of all was the great Earl William, Marshal of England. In 1211 he entertained King John at Pembroke Castle; the King had

Although Pembroke
Castle is a Norman-style
enclosure castle with a
great keep, it can be more
accurately described
as a linear fortification
because it was built
on a rock promontory
surrounded by water.

'come to Pembroke to cross to Ireland'. After William Marshal died in 1219, the Welsh under Llewellyn ap Iorwerth rose in rebellion. Other castles fell to the Welsh, but not Pembroke.

William de Valence became Earl of Pembroke in 1265. He added bastions and three gates to Pembroke's town walls. He also made great changes to the castle, defending the roughly hexagonal outer ward with six towers, one at each angle. He added a fine and impressive gatehouse, which had three portcullises. Henry VII was born in one of the rooms in the gatehouse in January 1457, which is why it is now known as the Henry VII Tower. Pembroke Castle was Henry's boyhood home for

14 years. William de Valence experimented with a completely new feature, a battlemented flying arch which joined two round towers inside the outer ward. It is not clear what this was for.

In 1400 the Welsh rose against the English again, this time under the inspired leadership of Owain Glendower. The Governor of Pembroke Castle was Sir Francis A'Court, who arranged for the payment of a danegeld to Owain Glendower, who in turn left Pembroke Castle alone. This was odd, because Pembroke was a very strong castle and could almost certainly have withstood Glendower's attack. One historian has called Pembroke 'the virgin fortress'; although the Welsh attacked and captured many other strongholds, such as Conwy and Harlech, Pembroke Castle was never taken.

In 1485, Jasper Tudor and his nephew Henry Richmond landed in Pembrokeshire; together with a force thousands strong and the support of Sir Rhys ap Thomas of Carew Castle, they marched to Bosworth, where they defeated and killed Richard III. Richmond became Henry VII by usurpation. His son Henry VIII gave Pembroke to Anne Boleyn. Pembroke was still in its heyday, a great working castle. In 1603 it was still a formidable fortress with 'all the walls standing strong, without any decay'.

In 1642, at the start of the Civil War, Pembroke declared for parliament, while the rest of the Principality declared for the king. In 1644, Royalist forces laid siege to Pembroke Castle, but the defenders were able to hold out until a Parliamentary fleet sailed into Milford Haven, lifting the siege. The castle stayed in Parliamentary hands until the 'First' Civil War was won. Major General Laugharne, who was then in possession of the castle, was ordered by Cromwell to dismiss his men. Laugharne refused and was imprisoned. The Mayor of Pembroke, John Poyer, garrisoned the castle himself and declared for the king. He was declared a traitor by parliament. Cromwell himself arrived with a huge army in May 1648 and laid siege to Pembroke Castle, setting fire to parts of the town. Poyer and Laugharne surrendered on 11 July. Their gentlemen-officers were allowed to go free but ordered to leave the country within six weeks. A military court condemned Laugharne, Poyer and Colonel Powell to death, but the Council of State decided that the death of one man would 'satisfy the ends of justice'. The three men drew lots and Poyer was executed at Covent Garden in London.

Then, with a sad inevitability, Cromwell sentenced Pembroke Castle to death too. He ordered its slighting. The barbican gate and five towers of the outer ward were blown up, together with the curtain wall of the inner ward. The ruins seem to have remained derelict until 1880, when Mr J.R. Cobb of Brecon launched a three-year programme of partial restoration. Then there was a further period of neglect. In 1928 Pembroke Castle was acquired by Major General Sir Ivor Philipps. He had all the ivy stripped from the castle walls, he had the trees and shrubs rooted out, and he undertook major restoration work. When the General died in 1959 his daughter leased the castle to Pembroke Borough Council, who took on the responsibility for conserving it.

Pembroke Castle is one of the finest castles in these islands. But it also has an curious secret. Under the keep is a natural cavern about 24 metres (80 ft) across, called the Wogan. It was entered by a staircase half in the rock, half in a turret. Leland said, 'In the botom of the great stronge tower in the inner ward is a marvelus vault caullid the Hogan.'

141

MANORBIER CASTLE

LOCATION **PEMBROKESHIRE, WALES**

DATE BUILT **12TH CENTURY**

FOUNDER **ODO DE BARRI**

Manorbier Castle is a graceful and elegant ruin, hiding in a valley near the sea. It has the distinction of being the only castle in Wales that was never attacked or besieged.

Manorbier Castle's founder, Odo de Barri, was one of the followers of Gerald de Windsor, castellan of the Norman fortress of Pembroke. Gerald had set up his personal stronghold and home at Carew, a few miles from Manorbier. Odo's son married Gerald's daughter Angharad and their numerous offspring became an important local family. One of their sons became a priest and achieved lasting fame travelling and writing, under the name Gerald of Wales.

Henry IV took the castle away from the de Barri family in 1399. The castle passed from one owner to another over the next 200 years. By the time John Leland saw it in the 1530s it was unoccupied and ruined. In the Civil War, it was occupied by Parliamentary forces, but was not besieged.

The castle is a single rectangular ward with no keep. It has instead a strongly built gatehouse and a well-preserved drum tower embedded in the walls. The buildings within the outer walls belong to the time of Henry II and Henry III, and include a lofty hall with a vaulted cellar.

Manorbier Castle was Gerald of Wales' birthplace, the place he loved best. This is how he described it in about 1180: 'The castle called Maenor Pyrr is excellently well defended by turrets and bulwarks, having on its northern and southern sides a fish pond under its walls, ... and a beautiful orchard, enclosed by a vineyard and a wood ... Towards the west the Severn Sea, bending its course to Ireland, enters a hollow bay at some distance from the castle. From this point of sight, you will see almost all the ships from Great Britain, ... daringly brave the inconstant waves and raging sea. The country is well supplied with corn, sea-fish and imported wines, and it is tempered by a salubrious air ... Maenor Pyrr is the pleasantest spot in Wales.'

Manorbier is a fine example of an early medieval baron's residence. Remarkably, much from that time can still be traced – the church, mill, pond, dovecote – very much as Gerald of Wales described it eight centuries ago.

SKENFRITH CASTLE

LOCATION **MONMOUTHSHIRE, WALES**

DATE BUILT **13TH CENTURY (ON SITE OF EARLIER CASTLE)**

FOUNDER **HUBERT DE BURGH**

Skenfrith Castle was one of three castles built within a few kilometres of each other to guard the routes in and out of Wales between the Black Mountains and the River Wye.

The Three Castles, sometimes known as the Trilateral Castles, were Skenfrith, White and Grosmont. To begin with they were made of timber; Skenfrith was later rebuilt in sandstone.

In the late 1130s, King Stephen brought the Three Castles together under a single Lordship so that the three fortresses could be controlled in a co-ordinated way as a single defensive unit. In the early 13th century Hubert de Burgh, Earl of Kent and Justiciar of England, held the Lordship of the Three Castles. He built modern stone castles at Grosmont and Skenfrith.

Skenfrith Castle was built on low, level ground on the west bank of the River Monnow at Abergavenny. The curtain walls make a big irregular quadrilateral with round towers strengthening each corner. Inside there was the usual domestic range, which included a hall on the west side. In the middle of the enclosure stands a small drum-shaped keep on a low grassy mound; in its present shattered state it makes a very fine picturesque ruin.

The lower walls of the keep are 'battered', deliberately inward-sloping, to give the structure greater stability and strength. There is also a semi-circular projection from the keep wall; this contained a spiral staircase that connected the three storeys inside the keep. After the round keep was built on the flat site, earth was heaped up round it, burying the lower storey and making it look as if the keep had been built on top of a motte, probably to make sure that the keep walls were properly founded on solid ground.

The Lordship of the Three Castles was granted to Edmund Crouchback, Earl of Lancaster, in 1267. Only Grosmont was used as a residence. As a result, Skenfrith stayed much the same as when Hubert de Burgh finished it.

The great days of the Three Castles were in the conquest of Wales by Edward I. Once this was accomplished, the Castles were not nearly so important. By the 16th century, all were abandoned and falling into ruin.

RAGLAN CASTLE

LOCATION **MONMOUTHSHIRE, WALES**

DATE BUILT **15TH CENTURY (ON SITE OF NORMAN CASTLE)**

FOUNDER **SIR WILLIAM AP THOMAS**

Raglan Castle is one of the most picturesque and romantic ruined castles. The first castle to be built at Raglan was a Norman motte and bailey. This survived until early in the 15th century, when Raglan came into the possession of Sir William ap Thomas.

Sir William was a Welsh knight who had fought at the Battle of Agincourt with Henry V in 1415, and like others doubtless returned with a self-image bursting with patriotic valour and chivalry; like other such veterans, he wanted a home that matched his self-image. In 1435 he started building the great tower, which is the oldest surviving part of the castle. This was a significant departure from the Norman concept of a keep, which was normally square or round in plan. Sir William's keep was unusual in being hexagonal in plan and surrounded by its own moat.

Originally the great tower was accessible only by a drawbridge from the main body of the castle; this has been replaced by a fixed bridge. It is said that the unusual defences of the keep reflect the owner's suspicious nature, enabling him to isolate himself from his own household in the event of a shift in their loyalties. It seems more likely that it was a defensive work more in the spirit of the fortress-within-fortress wards and baileys of other castles.

Lord Herbert, the son of the first Marquess of Worcester, installed an unusual contraption in the tower which frightened some commissioners who arrived to search the castle for arms. A hydraulic engine roared into life to raise a large quantity of water up to the battlements and pour it through the machicolations onto the heads of the intruders. The roaring sound echoing round inside the tower was quite enough to frighten the commissioners off.

The hexagonal shape of the Yellow Tower of Gwent was a way of reducing the vulnerability of the right-angled corners of the square keep, yet removing the extra difficulty (and cost) of making a curved wall. It was ingenious, yet it was not an experiment that was widely repeated elsewhere. The cream-coloured stone of which the great tower was built gave it its

The original Norman keep was an unusual hexagonal shape and surrounded by a moat. Access to it was by a drawbridge, which was later replaced by a fixed bridge.

nickname; it became known as the Yellow Tower of Gwent, which makes it sound like a location from a legend about King Arthur.

Sir William ap Thomas's son, William Herbert, Earl of Pembroke, continued the work of developing Raglan Castle, turning it into a high-medieval masterpiece. He added a great gatehouse and some lavish accommodation. The last important phase of building on the site was seen through in the middle of the 16th century by William Somerset, Earl of Worcester. He made improvements to the great hall of the castle. Even in its ruined state the hall is impressive. A large oriel window, once filled with heraldic stained glass, lit the high table, and the hall was heated in winter by a huge fireplace. The roof was supported by hammerbeams of Irish oak. Coats of arms and rich panelling covered the walls, and there was a minstrels' gallery above the screens passage at the lower end. It is easy to imagine Sir Walter Herbert entertaining Henry VII's queen, Elizabeth of York, here in 1502; her retinue included her own band, 'the Quenes mynstrelles'. Her husband, the king, knew Raglan well, as he had been sent there as a boy; it was customary for aristocratic boys to be farmed out to the households of other aristocrats, presumably to learn manners and independence.

In the English Civil War, Raglan Castle was held by Royalists, and paid the inevitable price. Even if Raglan might have looked more like a fortified mansion than a castle, it was given 'enemy castle' treatment when, in June 1646, it came under attack from a Parliamentarian army 3500 strong under Colonel Morgan. Raglan's misfortune was that it had been made the local Royalist headquarters. The Earl of Worcester, reputed to be the richest man in England, contributed vast sums to the Royalist cause; it was said that he kept all his money in the great tower. He entertained Charles I at Raglan on such a lavish scale that the king feared his visit would do more damage to the Royalist resources than an enemy siege.

After a heavy bombardment that went on for several weeks, the castle eventually surrendered, in August 1646, to Sir Thomas Fairfax, the commanding officer of the New Model Army. He had come in person to oversee the siege of Raglan. It was one of the longest sieges of the Civil War, a tribute to the castle's strength, and Raglan Castle was among the last of the Royalist strongholds to fall to Cromwell. The victorious Parliamentarians slighted the castle, but only with difficulty. It had been hard work taking Raglan Castle; now they had difficulty in knocking it down. After a major effort, they succeeded in knocking down two sides of the Great Tower by undermining them.

Sadly, they burned the earl's library, with its irreplaceable collection of old Welsh manuscripts. They also imprisoned the octogenarian earl, promising him that he would be buried at Windsor. He replied, 'God bless my soul, they will give me a grander castle when dead than they took from me

when living!' He did in fact die soon afterwards, and was buried in St George's Chapel, Windsor.

As elsewhere, further damage was done later by pilfering, which continued into the 18th century. The Duke of Beaufort ransacked Raglan for fittings for his new home at Badminton. The fifth duke called a halt to the damage and from that moment on the castle was preserved as a tourist attraction. The ruined shell of Raglan Castle is still a very fine and impressive building. As you approach its main gateway, it gives the impression of being complete. Many of the walls stand to their full height and the fine machicolations along the tower tops give it a distinctively finished and ready-for-action look. Only the window holes, like the eyeless sockets of a skeleton, speak of its ruination.

Raglan is like Bodiam Castle in Sussex, in being no more than an empty shell, yet a near-complete shell for all that, and still retaining the shape and majesty of the high-medieval castle in all its glory.

TINTERN ABBEY

LOCATION **MONMOUTHSHIRE, WALES**
DATE BUILT **1131**
FOUNDER **RICHARD FITZRICHARD**

Tintern is the best known of all the ruined abbeys in Britain. The surviving remains are substantial, they lie in a picturesque location beside the River Wye, and the visitor sees them against a backdrop of steep and densely wooded hillsides.

Unlike Fountains, where there are distant glimpses, we come across Tintern Abbey suddenly and without warning. The north side does not catch the sun and the dark masonry is gaunt and forbidding. But Tintern is powerfully impressive and has been a focal monument for Romantic poets and painters from Wordsworth and Turner on. When they saw it, it was a different place. There was no road beside it then, and the ruin had not been tidied up by a succession of well-meaning heritage bodies. The litter of carved and sculpted fallen stones lying on hummocky ground has been cleared away and the land levelled. Then there was ivy; now there is mown grass.

But there are always two views on conservation and presentation. There are those who want to smarten and restore a site like Tintern, which could easily be re-roofed, and there are those who want to allow it to go into a ruinous state. The Revd William Gilpin once argued that a few well-aimed blows with a hammer would improve the picturesqueness of the too-well-preserved gable ends. At Tintern I can empathize with both of those views. It is not entirely satisfactory as it stands, neither restored nor a picturesque ruin.

Tintern Abbey was one of the first great Cistercian communities in Britain, founded in 1131 by Richard FitzRichard, the Lord of Chepstow, in a secluded spot in the densely wooded valley of the Wye. The monastery was founded just a year before Rievaulx to house a community of Cistercian monks from the monastery of L'Aumone in Normandy. As a Cistercian house, the same austerity might have been expected as at the sister house in Yorkshire, but the church was rebuilt in the 13th century as the original one was too small; by the 13th century Tintern was rich and ambitious and the stone carving – Early English and Decorated – had turned opulent.

The Cistercian abbey of Tintern is one of the greatest monastic ruins of Wales. It was only the second Cistercian foundation in Britain, and the first in Wales, and was founded on 9 May 1131 by Walter de Clare, Lord of Chepstow. It soon prospered, thanks to endowments of land in Gwent and Gloucestershire, and buildings were added and updated in every century until its dissolution in 1536.

Much of the 12th-century phase of the abbey has gone during the course of rebuilding in the 13th and 14th centuries, so quite a lot of the early architecture has gone. Most of Tintern's documented history has been lost too because its records were destroyed when Raglan Castle was ransacked in the Civil War. But we do know that when Richard I was taken prisoner, Tintern had to surrender its wool production for an entire year as its contribution towards the colossal £100,000 ransom. It is also known that soon after its expensive rebuilding, Tintern played host to Edward II, who sheltered there for two nights before going on to his death at Berkeley Castle. In return for their hospitality, the doomed king granted the monks fishing rights on a stretch of the Wye.

Some time after this, the number of both monks and lay brothers at the monastery was drastically reduced, and that must have been because of the Black Death. The records are not there to prove it, but the reduction in staffing can only be explained in that way. Tintern may have been remote and isolated, but it cannot have escaped the effects of the Black Death, which is known to have swept through the valley of the River Severn in 1349, decimating the population as it passed.

Tintern Abbey's economy depended almost exclusively on agriculture, and probably made much of its money from the lucrative wool trade. This agricultural emphasis is underlined by the size of the lay brothers' refectory, which was significantly larger than the monks' refectory; medieval agriculture required a lot of human labour.

The abbey church is very well preserved, virtually complete apart from its roofs, window glass and tower. Its greatest feature is its west window, consisting of seven lights, and its fine stone tracery is best appreciated from outside the precinct. The nave, which dates mainly from the 13th century, still has a clerestory on its south side. The lovely arches at the crossing once supported a square tower, and beyond that is the finely proportioned east window.

The constraints of the valley floor site led the architects to place the large complex of cloisters and other monastic buildings on the north side of the church. To the north-east, beyond the cloisters and the rooms leading off it – library, chapter house, monks' frater – is yet another cloister garth, called the infirmary cloister. Beyond that again are the abbot's lodging and abbot's hall. Tintern Abbey made great use of the river as a waterway, and the adjacent hotel stands on the site of the abbey's watergate, where a 13th-century arch provides access to a slipway.

When the Dissolution came in 1536, Abbot Richard Wyche surrendered Tintern to the king's commissioners. The site was granted to the Earl of Worcester, but only after the king's plumbers had been over it to strip the lead from the roof and take the bells from the tower above the crossing. The monastic buildings suffered far worse than the abbey church itself. It was a shameful exercise in asset-stripping, wrecking both an architectural masterpiece and a useful economic and humanitarian institution, and it was an exercise repeated again and again round the kingdom. After this episode, Tintern's fate was to sink into quiet obscurity. Its remoteness protected it to some extent from robbing for building stone, though there was some small-scale robbing of stone for use in local houses.

Gradually the woodland stole back across the abbey site, and the ivy grew unbidden, turning it into a classic Gothic ruined abbey, just in time for the great vogue in Romantic ruins in the late 18th and early 19th centuries. Tintern Abbey became one of the 'must-see' sites for the Romantics. Turner's beautiful watercolours of the ivy-grown crossing are still among the definitive images, not only of Tintern but also of the Romantic movement.

CHEPSTOW CASTLE

LOCATION **MONMOUTHSHIRE, WALES**

DATE BUILT *c.* **1067**

FOUNDER **WILLIAM THE CONQUEROR**

Chepstow Castle was one of the first phase of Norman castles, built in the first five years after the Conquest in 1066. The building was overseen by William FitzOsbern.

The Normans set up their fortresses at Chepstow and Monmouth in preparation for the conquest of Wales. In 1093–4 they duly pushed on further into South Wales from Chepstow, building new castles at Pembroke, Cardiff, Carmarthen and Cardigan. Just as the Normans used their castles as stepping stones in the conquest of England and Wales, so Edward I, later on, used his castles to throw a ring of stone round rebellious North Wales.

Chepstow Castle was built on a hill, a spur of sandstone overlooking a river crossing on the Wye. Chepstow also had a harbour, which meant that it could be supplied by water from Bristol. It was also possible to send troops or materials by water upriver or along the coast to the west.

A substantial part of FitzOsbern's hall survives at Chepstow, along with the basic defences. They are even so only the nucleus of the massive castle built on the site by William the Marshall and later the Earls of Norfolk. Chepstow Castle saw further changes in the 16th and 17th centuries, but these were mostly minor alterations and embellishments.

Chepstow saw belated and rather futile action in the second bout of Civil War in the 1640s. The castles involved were commanded by officers who had changed sides in order to defend the monarchy. Chepstow was among a group of strong Welsh castles that put up significant resistance in this Second Civil War. It was a castle of the Somersets, where Sir Nicholas Kemeys commanded a garrison of 120 men. Cromwell built a four-gun battery, knocked down the battlements to deprive the garrison of its artillery and then demolished the curtain wall. After that the garrison ran off and Sir Nicholas himself was killed during the final assault.

In the 19th century the castle fell into neglect, lost its roof and was abandoned. Chepstow Castle as it now stands is a fine and substantial Gothic ruin, with weighty round towers, battlements and a fine gatehouse.

CALDICOT CASTLE

LOCATION **MONMOUTHSHIRE, WALES**

DATE BUILT **1221 (ON SITE OF NORMAN CASTLE)**

FOUNDER **HUMPHREY DE BOHUN**

Caldicot Castle stands on a site that had been recognized for its strategic value long before the castle itself was built. It was a good vantage point from which to watch ships in the Bristol Channel and easy to provision by water.

The Normans recognized the usefulness of Caldicot as early as 1086. They built a motte, two baileys and a deep surrounding ditch, and used the strong-point to control this area of South Wales. The motte is still a conspicuous feature of the site. The timber tower was replaced by a round stone keep in 1221, after Humphrey de Bohun inherited the lordship of Caldicot. The family held it until 1373, after which it became the property of the crown.

The four-storeyed keep with its local gritstone walls was a very strong structure that could withstand any assault imaginable in the early middle ages. The lowest storey of the keep was buried inside the motte, for structural stability, and the main entry point into the keep was by way of a staircase up the motte. Inside, the architecture was refined and elaborate and the accommodation was luxurious. The outside of the keep was, and still is, faced with finely cut smooth ashlar stonework. Running down the motte from the walls of the keep were stout curtain walls with round corner towers.

In the 13th century the castle's first gatehouse was installed; it still stands to almost its full original height. In the 14th century a timber great hall was added along the inside of the curtain wall.

In 1373, the last male de Bohun died and the castle passed to Thomas of Woodstock, Duke of Gloucester. He added the three-storeyed Woodstock Tower, installing a bath – a very rare refinement in medieval castles. His enjoyment of Caldicot was brief. He was murdered in Calais and the castle passed to his daughter Anne, who married Edmund Earl of Stratford. Later it became Crown property and was passed to the Dukes of Stafford.

The antiquary J.R. Cobb bought the castle in 1855 and restored it to its medieval state. He did a good job, producing an appropriate mix of the genuinely old and the carefully and authentically restored.

CAERPHILLY CASTLE

LOCATION **CAERPHILLY, WALES**
DATE BUILT **1268–77**
FOUNDER **GILBERT DE CLARE**

Caerphilly Castle is a veritable giant among castles; it is the biggest castle in Wales and one of the biggest castles in the whole of Britain and Ireland. It covers around 12 hectares (30 acres) of land, which means that only Windsor Castle is larger than Caerphilly.

The poet Tennyson commented, 'It isn't a castle – it's a town in ruins.' He was right. Looked at across the water, Caerphilly Castle does look like a small walled medieval city.

The site was defended by the Roman army as early as AD 75, when auxiliaries from the Second Augusta Legion stationed at Caerleon built a fort. It stood beside one of the main Roman roads, halfway between the forts at Cardiff and Gelligaer. When the Romans gave the site up, it was left abandoned for a thousand years. And when the medieval castle was built, it was designed and built all in one go, from the ground up.

When the Normans arrived in South Wales, they initially controlled only the fertile coastal strip, leaving the hill country inland in the hands of the Welsh. By 1263, a large area in South Wales was in the hands of Gilbert de Clare, Earl of Gloucester and Hereford and Lord of Glamorgan, one of the most powerful of the Marcher lords, the lords of the Welsh border country. Gilbert, known as 'Red Gilbert' because of his red hair, was a very influential figure, who gave support to Simon de Montfort in his campaign to reduce the power of the king. When Llewellyn ap Gruffydd was rewarded for supporting de Montfort with the title Prince of Wales, which gave him sovereignty over Welsh barons, Gilbert changed sides, going over to Lord Edward, who would shortly become Edward I. After de Montfort was killed at the Battle of Evesham, his son and supporters fled to Kenilworth Castle, taking refuge there. 'Red Gilbert' was among Lord Edward's supporters who attacked them there. He was able to observe at close quarters the impressive system of defences that surrounded Kenilworth Castle, and in particular the elaborate water defences which included a massive artificial lake.

The site was chosen because of its strategic position in the communications system; it guarded the entrance to several valleys, as well as sitting close to the old Roman road route from Chepstow to Brecon. From Caerphilly it was possible to command a great deal of territory.

Work started on building Caerphilly Castle in 1268, when 'Red Gilbert' de Clare, Lord of Glamorgan, became locked in a power struggle with Llewellyn ap Gruffydd, the Prince of Wales.

The design of this castle is a magnificent example of a medieval concentric plan; it is both the earliest and the best. A high and massive curtain wall surrounding the central inner ward is in turn surrounded by a lower and lighter outer curtain wall. That in turn is surrounded by extensive water defences, modelled on the water defences Gilbert had seen at Kenilworth. Caerphilly Castle was built in effect on three manmade islands; the large lakes round it were created by damming two streams. The curtain wall that flanks 300 metres (984 ft) of the town's Castle Street is actually a dam, holding back the water of the two streams on each side of the castle.

Llewellyn saw this large-scale castle-building project as a direct challenge to his authority, as indeed it was, and in the autumn of 1270 he attacked and burnt the half-built structure. De Clare started rebuilding at once. But then Llewellyn rashly challenged the authority of the new king, Lord Edward who had now become King Edward I. After a major Welsh campaign, Edward succeeded in defeating and killing Llewellyn.

The castle was more or less complete in 1277; it impressed Edward to the extent that he went back to London to rebuild the Tower on a concentric plan with a moat.

After Llewellyn's removal, Caerphilly Castle became more of an administrative centre for the de Clare estates. After Gilbert de Clare's son was killed at the Battle of Bannockburn in 1314, there was no male heir and Caerphilly Castle came under royal control until the future of the estates could be decided. A Welsh rebellion in the area brought an attack in 1316 by Llewellyn Bren with 10,000 men. This attack failed and caused no damage to the castle. Llewellyn Bren was captured and thrown into the Tower of London.

In 1317, the de Clare estates were divided among Gilbert's three sisters. The eldest of these

was married to Hugh Despenser, the favourite of Edward II. Despenser was greedy and unscrupulous, and tried to grab the rest of the de Clare estates from his brothers-in-law. In 1318, Despenser had Llewellyn Bren brought to Cardiff to be hanged, drawn and quartered, which only fuelled the hatred of the Welsh for Despenser. But Despenser's power at court grew until he was virtually king. During this time of power he built the great hall at Caerphilly Castle. Edward II's estranged wife Isabella and her lover, Roger Mortimer, landed a small army from France in 1326, which sent Edward and Despenser running for cover and for a time they took refuge at Caerphilly Castle. They were eventually captured and Despenser was executed in November 1326, while Edward II was forced to abdicate.

From this turbulent time on, Caerphilly Castle's role as a fortress of national importance declined. It also declined as a domestic residence. Its successive owners, who were multiple property owners, preferred the comforts of other properties. The castle fell into ruin and its stone was quarried for buildings elsewhere.

In the 19th century, with the Pre-Raphaelites and the burgeoning nostalgia for the middle ages, there was a move to conserve Caerphilly Castle and protect it from further ruin. The great hall was re-roofed in the 1870s. Between 1928 and 1939 John Crichton Stuart, the fourth Marquess of Bute, undertook the restoration of Caerphilly Castle. He had many of the collapsed buildings rebuilt and restored and re-landscaped the defence works. After the castle was taken on by the state in 1950, the consolidation and restoration of the castle continued. The reflooding of the lakes was completed, and the Great Hall of Hugh Despenser was restored. Today the castle is a major tourist attraction, with a collection of massive siege engines on display.

CASTELL COCH

LOCATION **CARDIFF, WALES**

DATE BUILT **MID-19TH CENTURY**

FOUNDER **3RD MARQUESS OF BUTE**

Castell Coch is a great Victorian masterpiece in medieval style. The architect William Burges created two castles for the third Marquess of Bute, one at Cardiff and the other at Castell Coch.

The Butes were an old and wealthy Scottish family with estates in Wales, and they became multi-millionaires in the 19th century as a result of the industrial development of Cardiff. The third Marquess was fascinated by the middle ages to the point of obsession, as was Burges.

Castell Coch was built on a site where that had once been a real medieval motte-and-bailey castle. Burges carefully followed the original ground plan, but he used grey limestone instead of the red sandstone used for the original castle. Above the ground plan, he followed his own instinct about the shapes and heights of the towers and walls. As a result the towers are much higher than they had originally been, and of unequal heights, which was probably fanciful. He also gave the skyline steeply pitched roofs, which were more continental than British in style.

Even so, it is very impressive, including the courtyard, which has no parallels in genuine medieval castles. The well is genuine and the murder holes above the gateway are authentic. The entrance gatehouse with its drawbridge has a distinctly central European look about it. Usually gatehouses and barbicans have twin towers. Burges characteristically gave his just one, but it is massive and surprisingly tall, with a fine conical roof.

Burges died before he could start the interior, though he left plans for it. His successors, who carried out his designs, toned them down. As a result, the inside of Castell Coch is less extravagant than Cardiff, but there are some genuine Burges touches. Lady Bute's round bedroom at the top of the main tower has a domed roof. It has a great bed of state decorated with crystal balls and also an ingenious dressing-table and washstand with porcelain towers containing water. This was not a Burges fantasy, but similar to the genuinely medieval example at Battle Hall in Kent. Lord Bute loved it all.

CARDIFF CASTLE

LOCATION **CARDIFF, WALES**

DATE BUILT **11TH CENTURY; STONE KEEP 12TH CENTURY**

FOUNDER **ROBERT FITZHAMON**

The occupying Roman army established a fort at Cardiff in the first century AD, enlarging it in the fourth century. In the 11th century the Normans built their castle on the same site.

Some stretches of the Roman wall were preserved and they were revealed during archaeological excavations in 1889. The Roman walls were rebuilt between 1922 and 1925 on their original foundations, which had survived.

The Norman castle had a motte as its centrepiece. Initially this had a wooden tower on top of it, but this was replaced with a stone shell keep in the 12th century. The structure was further reinforced in the two succeeding centuries by the De Clare family who owned Cardiff Castle. In that period the keep gained a gatehouse and forebuildings that were linked by a massive ward wall to a new tower on the south side, called the Black Tower. Sadly, these were demolished by Capability Brown during a redevelopment of the site in the 1770s. The moat that surrounded the motte was also filled in at that time, though later restored. Ironically, many landowners were building ruined castles to enhance their parks; here, Brown was selectively demolishing a castle to improve its appearance.

Richard Beauchamp, the Earl of Warwick, built a new tower and hall block on the western wall in 1423. In the late 16th century the Herbert family converted it into a well-appointed and luxurious house.

John Stuart, the third Marquess, spent large sums of money on building projects at his many properties, and in 1869 he started work on the remodelling of Cardiff Castle. The restoration was carried out to the designs of William Burges, a committed Gothic Revival architect. Lord Bute's great wealth enabled Burges to design and build his most fanciful schemes. The exterior was restrained, but the interior was fitted out in an ostentatious faux-medieval style. Some of the rooms are among the most remarkable of the Victorian era. Burges also rebuilt Castell Coch, not far from Cardiff, as a summer retreat for Lord Bute. These imaginative re-creations of the middle ages are close in spirit to King Ludwig's fantasy castle of Neuschwanstein.

ENGLAND

LINDISFARNE CASTLE

LOCATION **NORTHUMBERLAND, ENGLAND**

DATE BUILT **1542–50 (ON SITE OF EARLIER PRIORY)**

FOUNDER **BUILT ON THE ORDERS OF HENRY VIII**

Lindisfarne Castle, built in 1542, is one of England's most recent castles. Beblowe Crag on Holy Island is a perfect site for a fortress, overlooking the harbour.

Before the building of the castle, the island had never been fortified, but was given over entirely to the ecclesiastical activities of Lindisfarne Priory. In 634, King Oswald of Northumbria gave the island to Aidan, a missionary from Iona. Aidan was made Bishop of Lindisfarne in 635.

Lindisfarne Priory was one of the great holy places of the middle ages. The Normans called it the Holy Island and built a Benedictine priory on the site of the older monastery, which had been destroyed by the Danes. The remains of the priory – a fine piece of Romanesque architecture – are still standing to a good height.

In that older, Anglo-Saxon, monastery the monk Eadfrith devoted himself to producing one of the greatest art works that England has ever produced, the illuminated manuscript known as the Lindisfarne Gospels, finished in about 698. Before that, St Cuthbert was bishop here from 685. He retired to the total solitude of Farne Island, where he died in 687. His body was returned to Lindisfarne for burial.

The Anglo-Saxon Chronicle tells us that in 793 'terrible portents appeared in Northumbria' and the Danes drove the monks out. The monks took the body of St Cuthbert and later it was buried in Durham Cathedral.

That was the old Lindisfarne, but Henry VIII changed all that. The Dissolution of the monasteries meant the end of the priory, which naturally became a quarry for the new castle. The priory church was turned into the garrison's main storehouse and Lindisfarne Castle was completed in 1550.

The castle was never attacked. It was, however, briefly occupied by the French – for one night – and remained in a state of alert throughout the Napoleonic Wars. It was only after 1815 that its guns were removed.

At the end of the 19th century, Lindisfarne Castle was purchased by Edward Hudson, who commissioned Edwin Lutyens to reconstruct it.

ETAL CASTLE

LOCATION **NORTHUMBERLAND, ENGLAND**

DATE BUILT **1341**

FOUNDER **ROBERT MANNERS**

Etal Castle, at Cornhill-on-Tweed, started out as a medieval three-storey tower house. Unfortunately, it stood very close to the Scottish border, which rendered it liable to attack.

In 1341, the owner, Robert Manners, was granted a licence to fortify his house. What Manners then did was to create a square courtyard enclosed by a curtain wall, with the tower house in one corner and a substantial gatehouse in the corner diagonally opposite. The gatehouse was a big, solid structure with a portcullis, and it was originally defended by a barbican, joined to the gatehouse by a parapet walkway to the first floor.

The tower house itself was fitted with an additional storey and embellished with crenellations. Unusually, it had its own portcullis. The tower house is now only an empty shell. The overall effect must have been very impressive and powerful-looking. The curtain wall was nevertheless very thin by comparison with those of other castles, and it would have been very easy for any serious attacker to push through.

The Manners family was engaged in a long-term feud with a neighbouring family, the Herons of Ford Castle. This feud reached its climax in 1427, when it was claimed that John Manners, the heir to the Etal estate, had killed William Heron of Ford and one of his friends. The judgement went against Manners, who was required to pay 200 marks to Heron's widow.

In the early 16th century, the Manners family moved away, leaving Etal Castle in the care of a constable. In 1513, Etal fell to the army of James IV of Scotland during his ill-fated invasion of England, but James was killed nearby during the Battle of Flodden.

In 1549, Etal Castle was ceded to the English Crown, possibly to ensure that it would be upgraded properly. Etal was essential to the defence of the northern border.

The union of England and Scotland in 1603 changed everything. The Scottish border suddenly did not need to be defended at all. Etal Castle ceased to have any military value, and the neglect and decay accelerated.

BAMBURGH CASTLE

LOCATION **NORTHUMBERLAND, ENGLAND**

DATE BUILT **11TH CENTURY (ON SITE OF EARLIER FORT)**

FOUNDER **ROBERT DE MOWBRAY**

Alnwick and Bamburgh Castles, together with Dunstanburgh, form a trio of big powerful castles that in the late middle ages controlled the whole of north-east England.

Bamburgh stands in a spectacular location, on an outcrop of indestructible dolerite projecting like a pier into the North Sea. The dolerite is part of the Great Whin Sill, which is the largest intrusion of igneous rock in Britain and also makes the foundation of several key military defences; it is the same 30-metre- (100-ft) thick slab of rock that makes the inland cliff along which Hadrian's Wall was built.

The castle itself is made of red sandstone. It stands on the same site as a sixth-century fort which was the main stronghold of the kingdom of Bernicia, though nothing of this remains. It was in AD 547 that King Ida landed at Flamborough Head to begin the conquest of a swathe of eastern Britain from the Humber to the Firth of Forth. Bamburgh was at the very heart of this early kingdom, yet the early fort seems to have been a very unimpressive affair. Bede described Bamburgh as fortified by a hedge and a timber palisade. A Norman fort was built and in 1095 William II built a wooden counter-fort when he wanted to lay siege to the castle. Nothing much was achieved until Robert de Mowbray, who had escaped from the castle, was captured. William II threatened to gouge Robert's eyes out unless the castle was surrendered, so his wife Matilda agreed to a surrender.

During the 11th century, Bamburgh was gradually evolving and by the reign of Henry III the castle had become an extensive and well-established complex covering 2 hectares (5 acres). The castle site is narrow, in effect confined to the spine of the Great Whin Sill, and entered through an outer gatehouse with two flanking towers and a strong barbican. This leads to a succession of walled enclosures or wards. The fine big keep is an almost perfect cube 20 metres (65 ft) high. With its walls up to 3.7 metres (12 ft) thick it dominates the site and guards the Inner Ward.

Being so close to Scotland, Bamburgh inevitably became involved in the Border Wars. It initially stood up to bombardment well, but as weapons technology improved Bamburgh became more vulnerable. In the Wars of the Roses in the 15th century, Bamburgh came under decisive attack. After the Battle of Hexham, the Lancastrians were left holding only the castles of Bamburgh, Dunstanburgh and Alnwick – the three greatest castles of the north-east. Warwick 'the Kingmaker' and Montague, now Earl of

Northumberland, brought the massive siege-pieces of Edward IV to bear, and with these powerful new cannons set about crushing the last of the Lancastrian resistance in the north.

On 23 June 1464, Alnwick Castle fell to Warwick. The next day Dunstanburgh too fell. Now only Bamburgh was left, and Sir Ralph Grey, who held this castle, refused to surrender. He was exempted from the general pardon. Bamburgh was attacked with cannons by Warwick, and it was not long before chunks of masonry from the ramparts were blasted into the sea. Resistance quickly collapsed. It was the first time a battering ram was used effectively in England. The king's huge guns, called London and Newcastle (both made of iron) and Dijon (made of brass) made quick work of the walls of Bamburgh. Once they were breached, Warwick was soon inside the castle. Sir Ralph Grey was seriously wounded in this assault, but shown no mercy. He was dragged off to be accused before High Constable John Tiptoft, the Earl of Worcester, and executed.

That June, in 1464, Bamburgh won the doubtful distinction of becoming the first English castle to have its walls breached by gunfire. This significant technological breakthrough spelt the beginning of the end for all English castles as purely military strongholds. From that point on, the survivors increasingly became stately homes for aristocrats. Many of course did not survive, but were left in ruins.

After this disaster, Bamburgh languished in a state of disrepair for 300 years. During the latter part of her reign, Elizabeth I decided to give the tumbledown castle and its lands to the Forster family. Claudius Forster was a Warden of the Middle March (the middle route across the border into Scotland) and this was his reward. Claudius lived in the keep, amongst the ruins of Bamburgh, until he was 101 years old. Eventually the Forster family became bankrupt and in the 18th century had to sell both the castle and its lands.

The Bishop of Durham, Lord Crewe, bought the once-royal castle, with a view to repairing it and making it useful to the community. A windmill was built at the north end of the castle. The corn, which was ground here, was distributed to the poor. The bishop also set up a system of signals between Bamburgh Castle and Holy Island to protect sailors along this dangerous coast. In storms, men patrolled the beach, looking for salvage. There are still massive iron chains at the castle, which were used with shire horses for hauling beached ships up onto the hard, beyond the reach of the savage sea.

Bamburgh was acquired in the 1890s by the armaments millionaire Lord Armstrong. He rebuilt it over-enthusiastically in what he saw as baronial style, completing it in 1903. One architectural expert has commented that it shows 'the acme of expenditure with a nadir of intelligent achievement'. Bamburgh remains in the hands of the Armstrong family.

Archaeologists have made some exciting discoveries at Bamburgh. In the 1970s, Dr Hope-Taylor found 'The Bamburgh Beast', a tiny golden image of a fabulous animal. At 2.4 metres (8 ft) down, Hope-Taylor found evidence of human settlement – fish bones and carbonized seeds of grain – that were very old indeed. They dated not only to the time before the arrival of the Anglo-Saxons, but before the Romans. More recently, in 1998, a Durham University team explored the interior of the castle with ultrasonic scanning equipment. The idea was to search for man-made structures concealed within the ground. They found traces of ancient fortifications from the Iron Age. Bamburgh Castle is turning out to have a very long history indeed.

DUNSTANBURGH CASTLE

LOCATION **NORTHUMBERLAND, ENGLAND**

DATE BUILT **14TH CENTURY**

FOUNDER **EARL OF LANCASTER**

Dunstanburgh, Alnwick and Bamburgh made the north-east of England secure. But Dunstanburgh fell in the Wars of the Roses and, unlike the other two, has been in ruins for centuries.

The castle stands in an incredibly strong position, on a natural dolerite headland jutting out into the sea. The site was so effectively defended by the sea that walls were actually unnecessary along much of its perimeter. It is still difficult to approach. There is a walk of a mile and a half across moorland leading down to a hostile sea and the castle in dramatic silhouette – a fine view made famous by Turner's painting.

Possibly there was an earlier fortress on the site, but it seems more likely that Thomas Earl of Lancaster was developing the site for the first time when he built his fortress there after the great English disaster at the Battle of Bannockburn.

The Earl of Lancaster was the most powerful baron in England in the reign of Edward II. The earl and the king were in constant conflict, particularly over the favouritism shown by the King to his lover, Piers Gaveston. In the turmoil that followed Gaveston's assassination, the Scots seized the opportunity to invade northern England. This prompted the Earl of Lancaster to begin work on the great fortress at Dunstanburgh. It covers 11 acres, which is huge – large enough to corral all the people and cattle of the area if an invading Scottish army should pass that way.

The architect of Dunstanburgh, a mason called Master Elias, had worked under the great military architect and constable of Harlech, Master James of St George. Elias made much of his gatehouse (1313–25), which is large enough to contain the great hall and other state apartments, and built of the finest materials. The gatehouse had to be powerfully defensive but it also had to impress and intimidate.

Dunstanburgh was built on a grand scale. It had to provide space and protection for the local people and their livestock; the thick curtain walls and the steep sea-cliffs gave complete protection on two sides. It was was modernized in 1380–4, when the next head of the House of Lancaster, John of Gaunt, was Lieutenant of the Scots Marches. In the Wars of the Roses, the Lancastrian stronghold was besieged by Yorkists and fell in 1464; it was heavily damaged. It is still in ruins now, frozen in the moment of its surrender 500 years ago.

ALNWICK CASTLE

LOCATION **NORTHUMBERLAND, ENGLAND**

DATE BUILT **14TH CENTURY**

FOUNDER **PERCY FAMILY**

The market town of Alnwick (pronounced 'Ann-ick') is dominated by the magnificent castle built by successive generations of the Percy family, who were first Earls then Dukes of Northumberland.

The first Norman owner of Alnwick is thought to have been Gilbert de Tesson, William the Conqueror's standard bearer at the Battle of Hastings, but it is not known whether he raised any kind of castle. Yvo de Vescy became Alnwick's next owner, and it was he who erected the first elements in the castle that still survive. De Vescy died in 1134, and his castle was then described as 'very strongly fortified'. The Vescy line ended when William de Vescy was killed at the Battle of Bannockburn in 1314.

The Percy family was founded by William de Percy, who came to England with the Conqueror and was granted a huge estate extending across Lincolnshire and Yorkshire. The most famous of the Percys was Sir Henry Percy, known as 'Hotspur'. At 14 he took part in the Siege of Berwick and fought fiercely against the Scots when they invaded in 1388. Hotspur was captured by the Scots, and £3,000 of his ransom was paid by Richard II. He was also in favour with Henry IV, who gave him the castle of Beaumaris. Hotspur was killed at the Battle of Shrewsbury in 1403.

The original Norman design of Alnwick Castle can still be made out. In 1069, when it was new, it consisted of two walled enclosures with the motte, or keep-mound, in between. The two enclosures survive as the Outer Bailey on the west and Middle Bailey on the east. The motte would originally have carried a simple circular shell-keep, though this was later replaced with something much grander. The castle's more sophisticated style was developed partly because the Percys were constantly and incessantly at war with the Scots and therefore needed a strong fortress, and partly because of their high self-esteem.

When Henry de Percy acquired the castle and the barony in 1309, he rebuilt the original keep in a new style – seven semi-circular towers separated

Alnwick's gatehouse and barbican were built in about 1350. The battlements of the octagonal towers are topped by 18th-century versions of medieval human models, looking like a garrison of defenders.

by very short stretches of wall and tightly clustered round a courtyard. He also added the outer gateway and curtain walling fitted with imposing round and square towers. In about 1350, a gatehouse and towered barbican were added. The barbican, a pair of very fine octagon towers with battlements, bears a row of shields depicting the arms of the various families allied by marriage to Henry de Percy, the second Lord of Alnwick. Originally, there was a drawbridge in front of the octagon towers and a portcullis within, the groove for which is still visible.

Inside the arch and through a door to the right is a typical bottle dungeon. Beyond this door, the distinctive 'dog-tooth' mouldings of a very finely preserved early Norman arch can be seen. This was probably built by Eustace Fitzjohn in about 1150, and was left intact when Henry de Percy added the octagon towers two centuries later in 1350.

The extraordinary keep seems to have far too many towers and is far too big for its low motte. The octagon towers that form its entrance have their feet firmly on the flat ground in front of the motte. The overall effect is of a toy castle, though that is certainly not the effect the original architects intended.

The main entrance to the castle is on the west, through an imposing structure comprising a gatehouse and barbican, one of the most perfect of its kind in England. It was built in the time of the fourth Earl, the son of Harry Hotspur, in about 1440. Above the door is the Percy shield. There are also full-sized stone defenders, manikins quirkily added in 1764 on top of the gatehouse battlements. They look more like drunken guests at a house-party than defenders. They are in fact 18th-century versions of medieval manikins – a common ploy to fool enemy scouts into thinking the garrison was bigger than it really was.

There was once a moat, formed by the Bow Burn flowing along the south and east sides of the castle, but this is now filled in. Inside, there is a huge open space 100 metres (330 ft) across. This is the outer bailey, big enough to house an army.

In 1750, Robert Adam was commissioned to renovate the castle after many years of neglect, and this work went on until 1766. By then, Alnwick had been restored and transformed into a magnificent ducal residence in the fashionable new 'Gothic' style. To make the castle more imposing, the fourth Duke added the great Prudhoe Tower in 1854.

Alnwick Castle stands in a beautiful setting of what looks like natural, rolling English countryside. It is in fact a landscape designed by Capability Brown, complete with a lake at the foot of the grassy slope below the castle walls. The overall effect is evocative of the middle ages. The interior of the restored castle was furnished in a palatial Italian Renaissance style. The grand staircase leading from the entrance hall up to the guard chamber is startlingly incongruous. It is

If the castle seems reminiscent of *Harry Potter*, it's because it was indeed used as the very appropriate film set.

airy, ornate, with a blend of Carrara marbles. The guard chamber is pure Robert Adam.

The beautiful library in the Prudhoe Tower is in a similar style but warmed by red walls, red carpet and the gilded spines of 16,000 books arranged in two tiers; it has three book-lined alcoves with fireplaces, with a light gilded book balcony above. It is a spectacularly sumptuous room.

Alnwick is exceptional in every way. It is, moreover, still an aristocratic residence. This classic English castle was used as a location for Hogwarts in the first two *Harry Potter* films.

WARKWORTH CASTLE

LOCATION **NORTHUMBERLAND, ENGLAND**

DATE BUILT **12TH CENTURY/RECONSTRUCTED 13TH CENTURY**

FOUNDER **EARL OF NORTHUMBERLAND**

Warkworth Castle stands on rising ground above its namesake village in a loop of the River Coquet. Its impressive ruins are now managed by English Heritage.

The original Norman motte and bailey castle was built in the 12th century by Henry, Earl of Northumberland, who was also the son of David, King of Scots. In 1157, Henry II succeeded in retrieving Northumberland from the hands of the Scots and in 1158 he gave Warkworth to Roger FitzRichard.

In the 13th century a new castle was begun with the construction of a gatehouse. It is located at the centre of the south curtain wall. It has survived with its archway and semi-octagonal projections on each side, though it does not stand to its full height.

In 1332, the castle passed into the hands of the Percy family, the most powerful family in northern England and owners of nearby Alnwick. They made many major improvements to the old Norman structure, and built the great keep in the late 14th century. It is reckoned to be one of the finest keeps in England, with an advanced design that provided comfortable accommodation. The keep is polygonal, three storeys high, and it looks impressive from any angle. Unusually, the outer bailey was created over the site of the first castle. Within the outer bailey, various wall footings show the locations and shapes of the buildings of the original castle, including a chapel near the gatehouse, a solar, and a hall running along the west curtain wall.

The Percy family continually threw themselves into dangerous conflict with the English monarchy and the castle was returned to royal control on several occasions. Their influence was so great, though, that a family member was generally reinstated before long. Harry Hotspur and the third earl, his father, plotted to put Henry IV on the English throne.

The sixth Percy earl died in 1537, leaving Warkworth Castle and all his possessions to Henry VIII. After the execution of the seventh earl in 1572, the castle was pillaged by servants of Elizabeth I. After that disaster, Warkworth never recovered and it slid into decay and ruin.

PRUDHOE CASTLE

LOCATION **NORTHUMBERLAND, ENGLAND**

DATE BUILT **12TH CENTURY (ON SITE OF EARLIER CASTLE)**

FOUNDER **D'UMFRAVILLE FAMILY**

Most of the visible masonry in this fine ruin dates from the 12th century, though there was a still earlier Norman structure on the site. Prudhoe Castle has taken on many guises in its long history.

The castle has been a great fortress, a baronial home and a major administrative centre. Its situation in the Tyne valley, not far from the Scottish border, meant that it inevitably got entangled in the recurring border wars between England and Scotland in the middle ages. Prudhoe was at first owned by the D'Umfravilles, and only later passed into the hands of the Percys.

Prudhoe is laid out in a figure-of-eight shape. Curiously, its original inner and outer baileys are now separated by a Georgian manor house, on the site of the medieval domestic buildings of the castle. Inside the inner bailey the D'Umfraville family built a great tower, which stands three storeys high. Only the south turret still survives, but it gives an idea of the original appearance of the tower. The great tower at Prudhoe is its original keep.

Next to it was a range of 13th-century buildings, the 'forebuilding', the eastern wall of which was later incorporated into the 18th-century manor house. Further west, still in the inner bailey, are two round towers built in the 13th century. The one in the north-west corner is still virtually intact.

In the outer ward the great hall was the most imposing of the early buildings, though not much more than its foundations can be seen today. East of the great hall are the remains of kitchens and a 16th-century brewhouse.

The 12th-century gatehouse was a simple affair, a passage running beneath a series of arches. In the 13th century a chapel was built over it. The Percys aggrandized the gatehouse, giving it the first oriel window in England.

Prudhoe was still inhabited during the 17th century, but it had gradually fallen into neglect. In the 18th century it started to collapse. Early in the 1900s, the second Duke of Northumberland repaired and consolidated the walls that remained. The castle is still owned today by the Duke of Northumberland, a direct descendant of Sir Henry Percy.

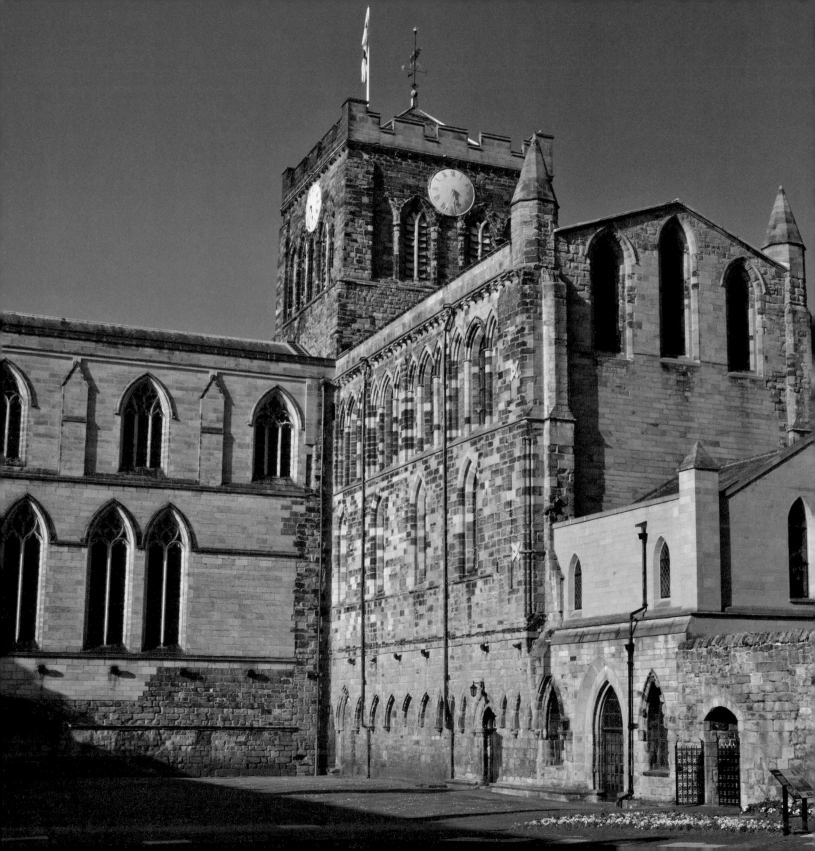

HEXHAM ABBEY

LOCATION **NORTHUMBERLAND, ENGLAND**

DATE BUILT **1113 (ON SITE OF EARLIER CHURCH)**

FOUNDER **BENEDICTINE ORDER**

Standing at the highest point of the town, the abbey church at Hexham is bigger than some cathedrals. The religious house was founded in 1113 as a Benedictine monastery.

Long before the Benedictine priory was founded, a church was built on the site in 674. Most of the stone for this building came from the Roman wall camp of Corbridge. The foundations of the apse of St Wilfrid's church still survive. There are also some fragments of the nave and the entire crypt, which is one of the finest Saxon crypts in England.

A major point of interest in the crypt is the deliberate use of carved stone from Roman buildings. It is possible that in the last quarter of the seventh century Saxon builders wanted to include significant references to the old Roman civilization, which they saw themselves as re-creating.

From 681 to 821, this great Saxon church was a cathedral with its own bishopric. In 876 it was sacked by the Danes. In 1114 an Augustinian priory was founded, lasting until the Dissolution in 1536. It was the Augustinian canons who built the existing choir and transepts. The transepts are unusually long, turning the church into an almost equal-armed cross. The south transept still has the canons' night-stair, which is very worn down by the feet of the medieval monks as they trooped down from their dormitory for services. The nave was destroyed by the Scots in 1296 and rebuilt as recently as 1908.

Hexham Abbey is richly furnished. The rood-screen, set up by Prior Smithson in about 1500, has 16 painted panels of saints and bishops. In the choir is the stone bishop's chair known as St Wilfrid's Chair. It may have been used as a coronation throne for the Kings of Northumbria.

The choir has some fine 15th-century misericords. The south transept has a Roman gravestone to a standard bearer called Flavinus, and also the Acca Cross, dating from about 740; St Acca was a Saxon bishop of Hexham.

Although the church has been lovingly maintained, the priory buildings to the south lie mostly in ruins. The cloisters lay to the south of the nave and west of the south transept, with the refectory to the south of the cloisters.

TYNEMOUTH CASTLE & PRIORY

LOCATION **TYNE & WEAR, ENGLAND**

DATE BUILT **11TH CENTURY**

FOUNDER **ROBERT DE MOWBRAY**

The history of Tynemouth Castle (whose gatehouse is pictured here) is closely interwoven with that of Tynemouth Priory, which is situated on the same rocky headland.

The site may have been occupied during the Roman occupation, and there is also a local tradition that it was used as a military base by the Vikings when they invaded northern England. Unfortunately, there is little to substantiate these claims.

Tynemouth Castle enters documented history for the first time in 1095, when we know that William II, William Rufus, succeeded in capturing 'Earl Robert's castle which is at the mouth of the River Tyne'. Bamburgh was taken at the same time. Earl Robert was Earl Robert de Mowbray, and his castle at this time probably consisted of an earthen rampart surmounted by a wooden palisade. Only later would the castle have been turned into stone.

When the nearby Priory was disbanded in 1538, the lands attached to it were granted by Henry VIII to Sir Thomas Hilton of Hilton. Tynemouth Castle nevertheless remained in the hands of the king. In 1545, a thousand workmen were busy fortifying the headland. Once the work was finished, a garrison of Spanish mercenaries was posted in the castle, and it became known as the Spanish Battery.

The castle played an important part in the Civil War, but then fell into disrepair. By 1681, it had fallen into a ruinous state and the defence of the strategically important mouth of the Tyne was taken over by another castle, the newly built Clifford's Fort at North Shields.

In 1900, Tynemouth Castle was a barracks and it had had many ancillary buildings added to it. In 1936, after the castle was gutted by fire, it was taken over by the Ministry of Works, who removed many of the additions and restored parts of the castle to something closer to their original form.

The great military strength of Tynemouth Castle really lay in the strength of its gatehouse. This is true of other castles too, such as Dunstanburgh, Bothal and Bywell. The gatehouse at Tynemouth consists of a rectangular tower with a projecting barbican – as at Prudhoe and Alnwick. People entered the castle by way of the barbican, along a vaulted passage protected by a portcullis and a gate, flanked by two towers. The basements of the towers functioned as guard rooms.

The open court beyond the gatehouse was originally a drawbridge pit (a dry moat) which separated the barbican from the gatehouse.

The gatehouse's first floor housed a magnificent great hall. This had a wide fireplace and was lit on all sides by windows. Next door is the kitchen with a wide fireplace and large oven. On the floor above the great hall is the great chamber.

At one time, the whole of the headland was enclosed by a curtain wall with towers. The western limb of this curtain is now mainly Elizabethan in date, but a fragment of the medieval Whitley Tower has survived. South of the gatehouse stood two towers, though these are now only earthworks revetted in stone for artillery. Much of the south wall was destroyed in 1851, though one of the medieval towers was left standing. The curtain walls on the north and east sides of the castle have collapsed into the sea.

The priory ruins are approached through a massive gate tower set in a fortified wall. Yet these are really the ruins of a religious foundation. For hundreds of years the ecclesiastical function paralleled a military function. The lofty headland guarding the northern entrance to the Tyne estuary must always have had a supervisory role. Even now there is a large coastguard station right next to the church.

A monastery had certainly been founded here by the middle of the seventh century. In 651, it is known from documentary evidence that Oswin, King of Deira, was murdered by his rival Oswy, King of Bernicia, and that he was buried at the Tynemouth monastery. Bernicia and Deira were the two ancient kingdoms of Northumbria. Miracles happened at Oswin's shrine. Oswin was declared a saint and the monastery became a centre for pilgrimage.

In the ninth century, its prominent location on the North Sea coast made it a natural target for Viking raids; it was attacked several times, in spite of its fortifications. The monastery was abandoned in 1008, and refounded in about 1090 as a priory of Benedictine monks; the refounding patron was Robert de Mowbray, the Earl of Northumberland.

Tynemouth's treasured relics of St Oswin were joined in 1127 by the earthly remains of Henry of Coquet, a local hermit-saint. Henry died of self-neglect, a kind of church-sanctioned suicide, in a cell on the small island of Coquet, which lies off the coast near Alnwick.

The monastic remains date mainly from 1090 to 1300, with the gatehouse added about a hundred years later. After the Dissolution of the priory in 1539, Tynemouth continued to be used as a castle, and the fortifications were added to in the 16th and 18th centuries.

Parts of the nave walls and the south transept of the Norman priory church are visible. At the end of the 12th century, the apse at the eastern end of the Norman church with its three radial chapels was taken down and the church was lengthened eastwards to create a presbytery in Early English style. Substantial chunks of walling from this structure survive, almost to their full height. It is easy to get an idea what the church would have been like when complete by looking at its fine, though ruined, west front, which dates from 1220–50 and still has its west doorway.

A peculiarity of the priory church is that a large chamber was built in the 14th century above the ceiling of the presbytery and choir. It is not known what this unique room was for. A small door in the middle of the east wall leads to the 15th-century Percy chantry. Its richly vaulted ceiling has 33 carved stone bosses crammed into it.

To the south of the church was the complex of ancillary buildings that were raised at every monastery and abbey. The cloister lay as usual to the south of the church nave, and the chapter house to the south of the south transept. To the south-west of the cloister and chapter house were yet more monastic buildings, including the dorter, the prior's hall and chapel, and the infirmary.

CASTLE KEEP

LOCATION **TYNE & WEAR, ENGLAND**
DATE BUILT **1168–78 (ON SITE OF EARLIER FORT)**
FOUNDER **KING HENRY II**

The Castle Keep at Newcastle was first a Norman timber fort. It was rebuilt in stone between 1168 and 1178, when it cost the substantial sum of £1,144.

The main focus of the castle was a cube shaped keep with a square battlemented tower at each corner; there was also a curtain wall, with a gatehouse near the south-west corner of the keep. The castle was added to in the 13th century, when an aisled hall was raised in the bailey. A barbican, known as the black gate, was added to the north gate between 1247–50.

Following the completion of the town wall in the 14th century, the castle was stranded inside the new defences. After that, the castle became redundant in military terms and in 1589 it was described as 'old and in ruins'.

In 1618, James I leased the castle to Alexander Stephenson, who allowed houses to be built within its walls. It was refortified during the Civil War and became the last stronghold of local Royalists when it was besieged in 1644.

The keep has been restored several times, most recently in the 1980s and is one of the best examples of its type in England. The accommodation consisted of one large room on each floor, with additional chambers, stairs and galleries within the massive walls. For defensive reasons, it was entered on the second floor by an external stair. On the ground floor is a chapel; the queen's chamber and museum are on the first floor, the king's chamber and great hall on the second. The roof offers a panoramic view of the city of Newcastle and the bridges over the Tyne, which the castle was built to defend.

The black gate is a remarkable structure. It is oval in plan with a central passage running through it, flanked by guard rooms. The lower half is in its original medieval form. The upper half was rebuilt in the 17th century, using the original stone; this is in effect a house built on top of the barbican, which looks absurd. In the 19th century the black gate was a slum, accommodating 12 families and a pub. The top floor and roof were later rebuilt when the building was occupied by the Society of Antiquaries. The name 'black gate' refers to the name of one of its tenants, a Mr Patrick Black.

DURHAM CASTLE

LOCATION **COUNTY DURHAM, ENGLAND**

DATE BUILT **1072**

FOUNDER **WILLIAM THE CONQUEROR**

Durham Castle was built on the orders of William the Conqueror, on his return from Scotland, and Waltheof, Saxon Earl of Northumberland, was given the task of building it.

Over the centuries the castle was continually rebuilt, but it is still dominated by its irregular octagonal keep with buttresses at the corners. What we see is not the original building, but one built in the 14th century by Bishop Thomas Hatfield, and then later substantially restored. The keep is set on a mound of sandstone, with its walls going right down to the solid bedrock. Through the middle ages it was, rather unusually, the bishops who maintained the castle; they treated it as their fortified residence.

Durham Castle turned out to be useless in a siege. When the northern earls rose on behalf of Mary Queen of Scots in 1569, they were able to take it without firing a single shot. For many centuries the keep fell into disuse. It was eventually rebuilt in 1838–40 to accommodate students; this was when the castle became Durham University.

The older part of the castle surrounds the keep on its high motte. This triangular courtyard or bailey is entered by way of a gatehouse close to the site of the castle moat, which was crossed by a drawbridge. The gatehouse was mainly the work of Bishop Pudsey in the 12th century, but later modified.

The Great Hall was built in the 13th and 14th centuries. Beside the hall is a very fine octagonal kitchen with three huge fireplaces, built on the orders of Bishop Fox in about 1500. It was one of the great castle kitchens designed by the military architect John Lewyn and one of only two to survive.

Palace Green separates the castle from Durham Cathedral. The buildings of the bailey, ranged along the edge of the cliff above the river, make one side of the triangle. Most of the houses in the bailey are Georgian, and they were very fashionable town houses in the 18th century.

Durham Castle has a fine setting, beside the town, palace and cathedral, on a high sandstone hill within a meander of the River Wear. Viewed together as a group, they make one of the finest architectural ensembles in Europe.

194

RICHMOND CASTLE

LOCATION NORTH YORKSHIRE, ENGLAND

DATE BUILT 1070s

FOUNDER ALAN THE RED

Richmond is one of the luckiest of the great English castles. Somehow, it managed to escape entanglement in any of the destructive maelstroms of English history.

Richmond Castle was begun in 1071 by Alan the Red, who was the son of a powerful Breton aristocrat, the Count of PenthiÀvre. The fort was built to command the entrance to Swaledale and the keep Alan built was one of the very strongest the Normans built.

The keep is a very imposing structure, a lofty double cube with four storeys, and the floor levels marked externally with discreet cornices where the walls step in a little at each successive level. There are four commanding corner turrets and some fine battlements. The great hall is the oldest building of its kind in Britain, apart from Chepstow.

Richmond stands on a spectacular site, a hill with a steep drop to the river bed. There are high moors on three sides, which made it very difficult for an army with siege equipment to reach it. It was virtually impregnable. The castle held a huge tract of the wild north under Henry II's control.

Richmond's one claim to a place in history was its use as a prison for King William the Lion of Scotland in 1174. Other than that there is no record of a siege or attack. This may mean that the castle was wrongly located, or it could indicate a measure of its success. A castle that nobody dared to attack or try to take had fulfilled its purpose effectively.

Its unprofitability was probably the reason it fell into decay. Medieval castles were expected to pay their own way by administering estates and dispensing justice. Being in a sparsely populated and poor area, Richmond made no money. By 1341, Richmond was reported to be in serious need of repair and also, ominously, 'worth nothing' in terms of annual income.

When John Leland saw it in 1540, he called it 'a mere ruine'. It says much about the strength of the original design and workmanship that, in spite of this long period as a ruin much of it is still standing. The magnificent keep is in mint condition, just as it was when it was built over 900 years ago.

WHITBY ABBEY

LOCATION **NORTH YORKSHIRE, ENGLAND**

DATE BUILT **657**

FOUNDER **KING OSWY OF NORTHUMBRIA**

Whitby Abbey stands on one of the most spectacular sites ever chosen for a great church – a high, windswept headland on an exposed coastline, giving the building a striking beauty.

The abbey was founded as a monastery in 657 by King Oswy to celebrate his victory over King Penda of Mercia. The Venerable Bede referred to this community of both monks and nuns at Whitby as 'Streonaeshalch'.

In 664 Whitby won a lasting place in English church history – as the venue for the Synod of Whitby. At this conference the method for calculating the date for Easter (which is still used) and other matters were decided. The Synod also decided in favour of the Roman over the Celtic church.

The first major English poet, Caedmon, was a monk at Whitby. According to Bede, he was an illiterate herdsman who in advancing years received a call in a dream to sing of the creation. He became a monk at the abbey under the supervision of St Hilda and turned biblical themes into Anglo-Saxon poetry. Hilda was baptized at the age of 13 by Paulinus and became abbess of Hartlepool in 649. She became the first Abbess of Whitby on its foundation in 657 and remained there for 22 years.

The monastery was destroyed by the Danes in 867 and abandoned for over 200 years. Then it was refounded as a Benedictine abbey by William de Percy. The abbey was finally dissolved in 1539. Although the domestic buildings were demolished, the church was allowed to stand, probably as a navigation aid to ships. In the 18th and 19th centuries much of it fell down and in the First World War the abbey was shelled by German warships.

Even so, enough has survived of the fabric to show what a splendid building it was. The chancel and north transept are still mainly intact, in Early English style. The east wall is especially striking, with three rows of windows with three lancets in each. Very little remains of the nave, though most of the surviving masonry dates from the 14th century. The cloister and the monastic buildings which lay to the south have disappeared. Remains of the buildings of the seventh-century monastery have been found by archaeologists.

BOLTON CASTLE

LOCATION **NORTH YORKSHIRE, ENGLAND**

DATE BUILT **1379**

FOUNDER **SIR RICHARD LE SCROPE**

Many of the castles in northern England have fallen into ruins or disappeared altogether after being pillaged by the Scots or destroyed in the Civil War, their stone plundered for other uses. Bolton Castle is unusual, just in having survived.

Work was officially begun on Bolton Castle in 1379 by Sir Richard le Scrope, who was granted a licence to crenellate his house by Richard II in that year. Sir Richard jumped the gun a little, as a surviving contract shows that the kitchen tower was built in the previous year.

Bolton was built at a time when castle design was evolving. The gentry wanted the security of living in a castle, but they also wanted a fine-looking house that would make an impressive show of wealth and prestige.

The gate-passage has a portcullis at each end, not only to prevent intruders entering, but to trap them. If they succeeded in reaching the square courtyard, they were still trapped. There are slots in the walls of the ground floor rooms, so that intruders could be shot down. The doors in the courtyard corners were protected by machicolations; boiling pitch could be poured on anyone below. These refined defensive features came at a price, and the overall cost of the castle was £12,000, a huge sum in the 14th century.

The Scropes' first connection with Bolton seems to have been in 1149, when Hugh le Scrope was a landholder in Wensleydale. The family fortunes rose after William le Scrope was knighted at the Battle of Falkirk in 1298. The Scropes were soldiers, lawyers and diplomats, and they amassed large estates in Yorkshire. Richard le Scrope, born in 1328, was a great soldier, fighting at Crécy in 1346, taking part in the siege of Calais with Edward III and the Black Prince in the same year. In 1371 he was created Baron Scrope and in 1378, under Richard II, he was appointed chancellor. Shortly after this, rivals challenged Scrope's right to bear arms, which was a calculated humiliation. At a hearing in Westminster Hall, Scrope was supported by the leading figures of his age, including Geoffrey Chaucer, who seems to have based his Canterbury knight on Scrope. The judgement went in Scrope's favour.

SCARBOROUGH CASTLE

LOCATION **NORTH YORKSHIRE, ENGLAND**

DATE BUILT **1135 (ON SITE OF ROMAN SIGNAL STATION)**

FOUNDER **WILLIAM LE GROS, EARL OF ALBEMARLE**

A Roman signal station stood on the headland at Scarborough. This was a tall stone tower 13 metres (43 ft) square and 30 metres (100 ft) high. On top was a semaphore signalling apparatus and a beacon-brazier. Today it's a much later building that stands here.

The Normans were the next great stone castle builders. After the great keep had been built at Rochester, Scarborough too got its own, smaller version, which was founded in 1135 by William le Gros, Earl of Albemarle. Both were thought to be impregnable. Henry II nevertheless proved otherwise. In a campaign to establish his authority, he destroyed some 500 castles. After he stormed the Earl of York's castles at York and Scarborough, the latter stayed in royal hands until the reign of James I.

Scarborough was a large royal castle, and Henry II saw it as one of the keys to holding the north. Medium-sized castles were used for the administration of law and order. To ensure their security, he needed the large royal castles as back-up; these included Scarborough, Pontefract, York, Richmond and Knaresborough. Together, this network of fortresses guaranteed him the command of the north of England.

King John was equally fanatical about castles, and he invested a large sum in repairing and reinforcing Scarborough, one of nine English castles in which he showed a special interest.

The only approach to the castle's headland site is from the west, and that is guarded by a strong barbican, a massive twin semi-circular-towered gateway with a flanking wall. The impressive curtain wall has 11 flanking towers, and it is dominated by the tall ruins of a shattered 13th-century keep. In the large outer bailey are the remains of the Roman signal station, two chapels and a medieval hall.

Scarborough Castle was besieged several times. In 1312, Edward II's hated lover Gaveston took refuge there and was starved into surrendering. In 1645, the castle was besieged by Parliamentarians, but they gave up and resumed their siege in 1648. George Fox, the founder of the Quakers was imprisoned there in 1665.

Scarborough Castle last saw military action, of a sort, in 1914, when it was shelled by two German battle cruisers. The damage done in these wars has been compounded by the effects of wind, rain, frost, waves and time.

RIEVAULX ABBEY

LOCATION **NORTH YORKSHIRE, ENGLAND**

DATE BUILT **1135–40**

FOUNDER **CISTERCIAN ORDER**

Rievaulx is one of the very finest ruins in England. Its soaring piers and arches spring from the green floor of Ryedale in such a perfectly picturesque way that it seems to have been designed as a Gothic folly by an 18th-century landscape architect.

It is hard to accept that, beautiful as it is, it was never intended to look like this. When the Cistercian monks chose the location for their monastery, they described it as a 'horror and waste solitude'. But the austerity and difficulty of living there was part of the attraction. The cramped site forced an unusual orientation onto the church, which has its axis twisted by that of the valley; the altar is to the south-south-east, not the usual east. Even so, there is an irony in the extraordinary beauty of the architecture of Rievaulx. It was supposed to be a plain building.

Abbot Bernard of Clairvaux wrote, 'What profit is there in these ridiculous monsters, in that marvellous and deformed comeliness and comely deformity? To what purpose are those unclean apes, those fierce lions, those monstrous centaurs, those half-men, those striped tigers? ... We are more tempted to read in the marble than in our service books and to spend the whole day wondering at these things.'

Not long after St Bernard wrote this, in 1131, the lord of the manor of Helmsley, Walter l'Espec, granted land in the Rye valley to the abbot and 12 monks who became the nucleus of Rievaulx, the first large Cistercian establishment in England. The Norman lord was a bearded warrior with a voice 'like the sound of a trumpet'. He entered the abbey as a novice himself, in his old age, then died there in silence after making his peace with God.

Within 30 years of Rievaulx's foundation, the third abbot, Ailred, presided over a spacious site occupied by a community of at

least 140 monks and 500 lay brothers. They built their abbey out of the sandstone quarried nearby and at Bilsdale to the north, and they built it all in a very short time. The nave was built in 1135-40, before any surviving Cistercian nave in France. In early Cistercian churches the aisles were kept separate from the nave by stone walling inserted between the huge piers, but at Rievaulx these walls were taken out in the 14th century.

By then, the chancel (choir and presbytery) had been built, in a less than plain style with stone-ribbed vaulting and some Gothic ornament. The columns and arches were delicately fluted, which created a sense of extraordinary grace and delicacy, like pale silken drapery. The floor was decorated with glazed tiles in yellow and green patterns. This eastern extension to the abbey church, almost as long as

The magnificent chancel with its fluted columns and tiers of arches is one of the most impressive features of Rievaulx.

the nave itself, was expensive, and it put the abbey heavily into debt. The chancel still stands virtually complete, with its three tiers of arches and even the arch of the crossing still in place; only the roof is missing. It is an architectural wonder.

There was a cloister, 43 metres (140 ft) square, which remains as a vast unenclosed lawn. To the east and south of the cloister lies a huge complex of monastic buildings, the warming house and frater, the day room, the novices' rooms, the treasury, the infirmary, the spacious abbot's lodging and the abbot's kitchen. The colossal scale of Rievaulx Abbey speaks vividly of the tremendous economic and cultural success of the monastic system – and of course of its unimaginable wealth. What organization today could afford to build on such a scale?

Rievaulx was isolated, but not isolated enough. Its location in the north of England made it vulnerable to attack by the Scots. It was also not sufficiently isolated to escape attack by the plague. By the time of the Dissolution in the mid-16th century, there were only 22 monks left at Rievaulx Abbey. The property was granted to the Earl of Rutland. A village grew up near the site, built out of stone plundered from the neglected abbey buildings. It is fortunate, for us, that the abbey was not close to a large settlement, as much more of the valuable stone would have been

carted off for re-use. As it is, the walls of the abbey still stand very tall in many places.

The chapter house, with its round apse, is an easy building to identify, even though none of the walls survive. It was built rectangular first, then the apse was added later. It was here, in the early years, that the abbots were buried. The gravestones of 13th- and 14th-century abbots can still be seen, together with the shrine of the very first abbot, who had been St Bernard's secretary and died in 1148.

The Dissolution took Rievaulx when it was already in decline. But when the abbey was in its heyday it was not only wealthy but teeming with activity. The monks attended their services, summoned by bells, studied in the library, tended their flocks of sheep, and warmed themselves on winter evenings in front of the two huge fires kept going in the warming house. It is easy to muse among the ruins and re-create all this in the mind's eye. In the 18th century, the poet Cowper considered moving to Rievaulx in order to do just that all the time.

Dorothy Wordsworth was equally taken with Rievaulx's beauty; she 'went down to look at the Ruins – thrushes were singing, cattle feeding among green grown hillocks about the Ruins … I could have stayed in this solemn quiet spot til evening without a thought of moving, but William [her brother, the poet] was waiting for me, so in a quarter of an hour I went away.'

These personal revelations followed Rousseau and Burke's discovery of the sublime. By the time the Wordsworths visited Rievaulx, the Duncombes of Duncombe Park had built the spectacularly imaginative Rievaulx Terrace in the course of landscaping their grounds. They created a long, wide lawn perched at the top of the valley side to make an enhanced viewpoint from which we can still look down on the magnificent work of the 12th-century stonemasons in the picturesque valley floor below.

HELMSLEY CASTLE

LOCATION **NORTH YORKSHIRE, ENGLAND**

DATE BUILT **13TH CENTURY**

FOUNDER **DE ROOS FAMILY**

Helmsley Castle is an early-13th-century fortress, apparently built by the de Roos family to guard the Rye valley, and to replace an older castle dating from *c.* 1100.

The early castle is thought to have been built by the founder of Rievaulx Abbey, which stands nearby. Helmsley Castle was one of a group of medium-sized castles in Yorkshire that were associated with hunting and the royal forests, even though they may have been in private hands.

Although it is badly ruined, it is still possible to get a good idea of its original layout. The inner bailey is rectangular in plan and enclosed by a curtain wall, which sadly has been largely destroyed. This bailey is guarded by round and semi-circular towers. The south barbican gave access to the inner bailey and was built as an outer gatehouse flanked by two round towers.

The south gate is badly ruined, but it is still possible to see the slot for the portcullis on the west side. To the north of the inner bailey, only the basements of the two gate towers have survived. Beyond that, the north barbican formed an outer gate; this too was flanked by round towers. Halfway along the east curtain wall stands the D-shaped east tower, which may have functioned as the castle's keep. It was first built in the 12th century and later modified. The join between the older lower stonework and the later sandstone upper levels is visible.

In the Civil War, Helmsley Castle was held by Royalist forces and finally surrendered to the Parliamentarians after a long siege. As a result it was severely slighted after the siege. The Tudor mansion built next to the west tower of the castle somehow survived this slighting more or less intact.

Part of the charm of Helmsley Castle is the fact that there are substantial traces of all of the various phases of the castle's history, from the early earthworks surrounding the inner bailey to the great Elizabethan remodelling of the west range and the systematic destruction after the Civil War siege. Helmsley is no longer the forbidding and threatening fortress it was in the middle ages, but a picturesque ruin.

FOUNTAINS ABBEY

LOCATION **NORTH YORKSHIRE, ENGLAND**

DATE BUILT **1135–47**

FOUNDER **BENEDICTINE/CISTERCIAN ORDERS**

Fountains Abbey, which stands in beautiful wooded countryside three miles south-west of Ripon, is one of the three greatest ruins in England. It ranks with Stonehenge and Hadrian's Wall in international celebrity.

The early days of Fountains Abbey were architecturally unpromising, as it was a Cistercian house, and Cistercian monks preferred austerity and stark simplicity. The site too was a lonely and forbidding spot in the Skell valley, 'fit rather to be the lair of wild beasts than the home of human beings'. The abbey was founded in 1132 by Benedictine monks who were dissatisfied with St Mary's Abbey in York, where they believed that the rules of their order were not applied strictly enough. Bernard of Clairvaux, who was the champion of Cistercian reform, sent the breakaway monks encouraging letters and Archbishop Thurstan granted them land in Skelldale where the first modest timber shelters were built.

The new abbey took its name from a Latin description, Sancta Maria de Fontanis. All Cistercian foundations were dedicated to St Mary the Virgin, so it was 'Fontanis' ('of the springs'), that became the identifying tag. The Skell too got its (Saxon) name from the springs rising on the valley sides nearby.

The stone building was begun in 1135, in Romanesque style, on a surprisingly grandiose scale and used the local sandstone. Its pale shades of pink, fawn, brown and grey are of the place and perfectly fit both the landscape and the architecture. The design followed the Cistercian rule – plain and unornamented, with thick round piers and round arches. There are also some pointed arches; it was the Cistercians who introduced this Gothic feature into England. The nave and transepts of the church were built first (1135–47), then the rebuilt domestic buildings (1147–79), then the rebuilt east end of the church (1220–47).

In 1147, at the climax of an unseemly row between the abbot and the Archbishop of York, much of Fountains Abbey was deliberately burnt down in a revenge attack by the Archbishop's knights. The building was gradually repaired. The rebuilding included a new east transept called the Chapel of the Nine Altars, which has incredibly high slender pillars, lancet windows and arcades on all sides. Even though now ruined, this chapel is still one of the architectural wonders of Europe. The octagonal piers have decorated capitals and originally had shafts of black spotted marble. All this is a long way from the original Cistercian conception of what the building should be. Evidently increasing wealth was having a softening and corrupting effect. By the Dissolution, any pretence at a strict Cistercian code had long gone.

Like other abbeys, Fountains was the economic hub of its locality. Its production and export of wool brought new prosperity to medieval Yorkshire, and helped the north to recover after William I's 'harrying of the north'. By the middle of the 13th century, Fountains was the richest Cistercian abbey in England, owning wool-producing estates throughout the huge county of Yorkshire.

LEFT Fountains Abbey is an outstanding example of the skills employed by the 12th-century lay brethren, and is an unrivalled feat of medieval architecture.

RIGHT Flying buttresses support the refectory roof.

One of the wonders of Fountains Abbey is the tall tower in Perpendicular style built by Abbot Huby in 1500–20. The Cistercians had always banned steeples and towers as extravagances and displays of vanity, but now Fountains had a splendid tower.

When Fountains Abbey was dissolved, its lead, glass and furnishings were taken by Henry VIII. The property passed through many hands and some of the buildings were demolished for stone to build the nearby mansion. But the depredations had not gone too far when, in 1768, Fountains passed into the ownership of William Aislaby, who lived at the nearby estate of Studley Royal Park. By this time, there was a 'Gothick' interest in noble ruins. Many landowners were building fake ruins. Aislaby acquired the real ruins of Fountains and developed the grounds around them to create a fine setting for them. What he created was a truly sublime romantic landscape. It was fortunate that Fountains Abbey fell into the hands of such an enlightened owner. It is thanks to William Aislaby that so much of it is still standing today.

The nave is well preserved, a fine example of austere Cistercian architecture. It is 11 bays long and stands to its full original height; only the roof is missing. It is a pity that funding cannot be found to re-roof Fountains, to ensure its future survival.

One of the finest features of the abbey is the undercroft or cellarium under the monks' dormitory. This runs for 91 metres (300 ft) southwards from the western end of the church, along the side of the cloister and across to the river. It is almost as long as the abbey church itself, and divided down the centre by a columned arcade; there are 19 columns, which sprout, unusually without capitals, into perfectly intact quadripartite stone vaulting. The arches at the church end are rounded. Those at the other end are pointed, showing that the structure was built across the boundary between the Romanesque and Early English styles. It may be that the Romanesque section survived the fire, and the southern section had to be rebuilt. The water supply and drainage system were complex and their remains can still be seen.

In fact, many thousands *do* come to see the many wonders of Fountains Abbey. It is no longer 'remote from all the world', which is what the founding monks were looking for, but a magnet for tourists from all over the world. The best approach to Fountains Abbey is from the north-east, walking as William Aislaby did, from Studley Park, now a National Trust property, by the banks of the River Skell. From this direction, the visitor comes suddenly on an evocative and tantalizing distant view of the ruined abbey.

CONISBROUGH CASTLE

LOCATION **SOUTH YORKSHIRE, ENGLAND**

DATE BUILT **1180**

FOUNDER **HAMELIN PLANTAGENET**

The name 'Conisbrough' is derived from Anglo-Saxon and means 'the defended *burh* of the king', suggesting that this was a fortified site before the Norman Conquest.

The castle was built in 1180 by Hamelin Plantagenet, the illegitimate half-brother of Henry II. In 1164, Hamelin married Isabel, the Warenne heiress who had inherited the manor together with its early Norman timber-built castle. What Hamelin built at Conisbrough was the very latest in military architecture – a cylindrical keep within a small single bailey all built on top of the motte. The curtain wall has round wall-towers at the angles. At 27 metres (90 ft) high, the keep was a good deal higher than normal. Because of its height, Hamelin added six enormous projecting buttress-towers.

The keep is attached to the curtain wall at its strongest point, with one side exposed to the field; this meant that, in the event of total disaster – a successful siege – the garrison stood some chance of escaping. The keep is faced with pale limestone ashlars, all still in place, giving the structure a peculiarly modernistic look. This startling effect is exaggerated by the scarcity of windows; it must have been a desperately dark and oppressive building to live in, though the interior was doubtless whitewashed to maximize the light.

The keep's interior was, even so, built with comfort in mind. It has the two earliest known hooded fireplaces in England. There is a wide staircase with shallow steps. There are water cisterns at the upper levels, so that the inhabitants did not have to go down to ground level to fetch water. There was also a pigeon loft, which was part of the Norman postal network. Later, the inner bailey's curtain wall and other buildings were added, but the masonry of these lesser structures is not to the same standard.

Conisbrough Castle stands between Doncaster and Rotherham, in an industrial landscape. The castle nevertheless attracted the eye of Sir Walter Scott, who used it as background for his great romantic novel *Ivanhoe*.

BEESTON CASTLE

LOCATION **CHESHIRE, ENGLAND**

DATE BUILT **1220**

FOUNDER **RANDULPH DE BLUNDEVILLE, EARL OF CHESTER**

Just to the south of Tarporley, Beeston Castle perches on the edge of a tall sandstone precipice, peering down at the Cheshire Plain, which lies spread out like a map, far below.

Beeston looks impregnable. Yet its spectacular location belies its history. In the long saga of its 800-year-long story, Beeston Castle has been captured several times – and slighted twice over. It is not nearly as invincible as it looks.

The entrance to the castle is at the foot of the hill, and there is a climb past the masonry of the outer bailey. A modern footbridge across a deep ditch cut through solid bedrock replaces the medieval drawbridge, giving access to the inner ward. The semicircular towers of the inner gatehouse lead on to the highest, innermost area of the castle, right on the brink of the precipice.

Not much is left there, but there are stumps of very thick walls in crudely worked sandstone that show that it must once have been a very strong fortress.

Beeston Castle was built in 1220 by Randulph de Blundeville, Earl of Chester. Unusually, he never built a keep at Beeston, but instead raised a long curtain wall to enclose the sloping outer bailey. If an enemy force climbed that far, it would then be confronted by the great ditch and the rocky inner defences. After heavy rain, even standing on these muddy slopes, let alone fighting in full armour, would be difficult enough. Probably the easiest way to take the castle was to make a direct assault on the rocky cliff, and this may be why in the Civil War a Royalist officer took that route into the stronghold.

The castle was already in ruins by the start of the 16th century. It had been the focus of a battle between king and barons in Simon de Montfort's time, and then again in the Wars of the Roses. After that it was rebuilt and strengthened, changing hands during the Civil War in the 17th century.

It was finally besieged in 1646 by Cromwell's army after holding out for four months. Then the food supplies were exhausted and they were forced to surrender, though they were not short of water, which was drawn from a very deep well cut down through the sandstone within the castle.

NEWARK CASTLE

LOCATION **NOTTINGHAMSHIRE, ENGLAND**
DATE BUILT **12TH CENTURY (ON SITE OF EARLIER CASTLES)**
FOUNDER **BISHOPS OF LINCOLN**

Newark is at a crossing-place on the River Trent where road and river routes converge. It was strategically important from the earliest times; the routes were in use in prehistory.

Roman defences were built at this site, and these were replaced in about 900 by the 'New Work' which gave the town its name. These Saxon defences were raised against the Danes.

The Norman castle therefore had a succession of predecessors. Early in the 12th century, Newark fell under the ownership of the bishops of Lincoln, and it was they who built the very fine stone castle that was described in 1138 by Henry of Huntingdon as 'magnificent and of very ornate construction'.

This ruin of a magnificent castle occupies a low yet commanding position by the River Trent, which makes a natural moat along one side. During the middle ages, the castle was added to and modernized. By the time of the Civil War, it was one of the most powerful castles in England.

In 1642, the Royalist generals decided to garrison and fortify Newark Castle and make it the centre of a large fortified area that could be used as a supply centre and rallying point for Royalist armies. They Royalists needed to retain control of the point where the Great North Road crossed the Trent in order to keep communication open between Charles I's headquarters in Oxford and Newcastle where his arms convoys from the Netherlands landed.

The Parliamentarians made three attempts to take Newark. The first two – in 1643 and again in 1644 – were unsuccessful. The third siege, in 1645–6, was by a joint English-Scots force of 16,000, commanded by General Poyntz. This time a great battering-fort called Edinburgh was used, as well as two bridges of boats. Eventually Newark was reduced to 'a miserable, stinking, infected town' and the Royalist defenders were forced to surrender. The siege of Newark was the last major action of the First Civil War; inevitably, Oxford too surrendered within a few weeks.

Since the 17th century, Newark Castle has stood in ruins but it is still very imposing and gives a striking impression of its former strength.

TATTERSHALL CASTLE

LOCATION **LINCOLNSHIRE, ENGLAND**

DATE BUILT **1440s**

FOUNDER **LORD CROMWELL**

In the 15th century, a new fashion developed for what has been called 'bastard feudalism'. It involved the addition of very capacious towers, large enough for the feudal lord and his retainers to live in, embedded in the castle's curtain wall. The finest example of this style is Tattershall Castle.

Like Bodiam Castle, Tattershall was rescued and restored back to its medieval state. Tattershall Castle's rescuer was Lord Curzon, who bought it in 1911, restored it and left it to the National Trust in 1925.

Henry VI's Treasurer, Lord Cromwell, became one of the richest men in England. It seems that much of his wealth was acquired dishonestly. In his will dated 1455 he left his executors the task of paying back, 'for conscience's sake', over £5,000 which he had extorted from various people. At Tattershall in Lincolnshire he built and endowed a magnificent church where he asked for perpetual prayers to be said for his soul. It stands next to the castle.

The huge tower, which still stands intact, was erected on the west side of the inner bailey of a 13th-century castle. It is grotesquely oversized for the bailey, and looks strange without the curtain wall. Nearly everything but the tower has gone, but clearly the overall defence works were impressive.

There is a vaulted basement in the tower, and four storeys above that, the whole structure standing 37 metres (120 ft) high. The three upper storeys were Cromwell's accommodation, with spiral staircases, splendid fireplaces and traceried windows. It is clear that Cromwell lived here in great style. It looks as if he built for show rather than security. There are battlements and a moat, it is true, but there are three entrances, all of them weakly defended.

What Lord Cromwell built at Tattershall was not so much a castle as a palace that looked like a castle – hence the term 'bastard feudalism'. This was really a grandiose version of the little moated manor houses that were springing up all over England, the homes of lords and even knights who wanted to live out the fantasy of living in castles. But the age of castles was over – though it took the Civil War, and another Cromwell, to prove it.

BELVOIR CASTLE

LOCATION **LEICESTERSHIRE, ENGLAND**
DATE BUILT **1080s**
FOUNDER **ROBERT DE TODENI**

Belvoir Castle is now more a mansion than a fortress. It nevertheless began life as a true castle, an earth and timber fort raised in the years after the Norman Conquest.

The castle was built by Robert de Todeni, who served as William the Conqueror's standard bearer at the Battle of Hastings. The simple motte castle (a keep on a mound) that stood on the site in the 1080s was typical of those being raised all over England at that time. Not much is known of the initial fortification, but the early timber castle was replaced in stone. A medieval seal shows the castle with a big rectangular keep and a masonry curtain wall surrounding it.

Robert de Todeni also built a priory next to his castle. His descendants were the Albini family. When the last male Albini heir died in 1247, Belvoir Castle (a Norman French name meaning 'beautiful view', but now pronounced 'Beaver') passed through marriage to Robert de Ros. The de Ros family kept the castle until 1464, when Thomas, Lord Ros, was executed for supporting the Lancastrians in the Wars of the Roses. After that, Belvoir Castle passed to William, Lord Hastings. Sadly, it fell into a ruinous state after an attack by friends of Lord Ros and then quarrying by Lord Hastings.

After Henry VII seized the throne, Belvoir Castle was once again granted to the de Ros family. Thomas Manners, first Earl of Rutland, instigated the castle's rebirth in 1523; it was completed 32 years later by the second earl. What emerged was a typical Tudor mansion, a lightly fortified manor house. From that time on, Belvoir Castle has remained in the hands of the Rutlands, first earls and later dukes.

This Tudor structure was also destroyed, in the Civil War. A new castle was raised on the site, between 1654 and 1668. Remarkably, the Belvoir Castle we see today is not even this Stuart castle but yet another rebuild! Much of the 17th-century castle was torn down and not rebuilt until the 19th century. A fire devastated the structure in 1816, yet still the castle was revived.

In spite of all these destructions, Belvoir Castle is today a magnificent stately home, though in questionable taste. The exterior is a profusion of architectural shapes modelled in cream and orange stone. The interior is equally sumptuous.

CASTLE RISING

LOCATION **NORFOLK, ENGLAND**
DATE BUILT *c.* **1140**
FOUNDER **WILLIAM D'ALBINI**

Two mysterious royal deaths are linked with Castle Rising. The first is the death of Henry I in 1135. He was said to have died 'of a surfeit of lampreys' – probably food poisoning. The second concerns the murder of Edward II.

Two years after Henry I's death, his widow, Queen Adelaide of Louvain, married William d'Albini, the Earl of Arundel. He built a fine castle at Castle Rising to mark his promoted status as consort of the Queen of England.

Castle Rising is a backwater now, but then it was a place of some consequence. A local verse has it that: 'Rising was a seaport when Lynn was but a marsh. Now Lynn it is a seaport town and Rising fares the worse.' The recession of the sea left the old port stranded.

The fine old castle rises from massive earthworks. There is a very deep ditch with a high rampart on the inner side, and this surrounds a circular bailey. In the bailey squats a great square unroofed keep. This is a very fine piece of Norman architecture, with a great deal of ornamental stonework on the outside. There were several rooms on each of the original two floors, and the entrance was at first-floor level, reached by an external stone staircase.

In the 14th century, Castle Rising became the property of Edward III, who installed his mother Isabella there after the execution of her lover, Roger Mortimer. This is where the second royal death enters Castle Rising's story: the murder at Berkeley Castle of Edward II. There is no proof that the assassins were acting on direct orders from Edward's wife, Isabella, but the circumstantial evidence is overwhelming.

In those days, the keep did not stand on its own in the bailey, but was surrounded by other ancillary buildings. The castle would have looked – and functioned – like a miniature medieval town. There were granaries, stables, a chapel and lodgings. All of these buildings have gone. There is now but a fragment of the Norman gatehouse still standing near the tower.

By the reign of Edward IV, Castle Rising was said to have 'no room in it but let in rain, wind and snow' – an apt description of its present state.

CASTLE ACRE

LOCATION **NORFOLK, ENGLAND**
DATE BUILT *c.* **1090**
FOUNDER **WILLIAM DE WARENNE**

The priory at Castle Acre has withstood the ravages of time and tyrant better than the castle. The priory is the most important Cluniac ruin in England; it is also the most impressive ruin of any kind in East Anglia.

The castle was probably built by William de Warenne, the same Warenne who built the castle at Lewes, and who introduced the Cluniac order into England.

The architecture at the Cluniac priory was lavish by comparison with the austere Cistercian houses; the Cluniacs were renowned for their elaborate church services. The west front of the priory stands almost to its full height. Its Norman doorway, with four orders of columns and intricate mouldings, is flanked by smaller doorways. The stone is brown sandstone. Over the main door a big Gothic window was inserted in the 15th century.

Behind this façade, only fragments remain. There was an aisled nave and a central tower that stood on four massive stone-encased piers, now just weathered remnants of broken arches and soaring towers of flint.

During Edward I's reign, Castle Acre Priory was fortified against Benedict, who had been appointed prior in place of the 'sitting tenant', William of Shoreham. The retainers of the lord of the manor came to William's aid, and saw off the intruder.

In 1537, the priory was dissolved and the buildings became a stone quarry for all the builders in the area. Much of the ashlared facing stone was taken, leaving only the flint rubble cores of the walls. The land passed through the hands of the Duke of Norfolk and then, after his disgrace and execution, into those of Thomas Gresham, one of Elizabeth I's favourites. The Cecils became owners and finally the Coke family. Under the latter, parts of the west range, once the prior's lodging, were turned into a dwelling house.

The ruins of Castle Acre Priory stand at the edge of the village, which lies within the huge outer bailey of the castle. The site lies on the ancient course of the Peddars Way. It is very hard to visualize what they looked like in their heyday – but they were certainly large and impressive buildings.

OXBURGH HALL

LOCATION **NORFOLK, ENGLAND**
DATE BUILT **1482**
FOUNDER **SIR EDMUND BEDINGFIELD**

In 1482 Sir Edmund Bedingfield was granted his licence to crenellate Oxburgh by King Edward IV. He built the moated manor house that he coveted as a fashionable status symbol.

Since Sir Edmund's day there have been a few changes, including the demolition of the Great Hall in 1775, and extensively remodelling in the 19th century. At that time the house was lavishly enhanced with a suite of fake Tudor rooms; outside, some pretty oriel windows, bay windows and fancy twisted chimneys in terracotta have given the building a distinctly Gothic appearance, but the underlying structure is still the late-15th-century one.

Oxburgh Hall has been the home of the Bedingfield family since well before the present house was built, and there are still family members living there. In the 16th and 17th centuries, the Bedingfields were repeatedly persecuted for their Catholicism, though they steadfastly remained loyal to the Crown. In 1487 Henry VII visited Oxburgh Hall, and since then the room he slept in has naturally been called the king's room.

Oxburgh contains many interesting features, including a fine parterre garden and a walled Victorian kitchen garden. There is a magnificent spiral staircase made of brick, leading from the armoury up to the roof. In a small room next to the king's room are preserved the embroidered wall hangings made by Mary Queen of Scots during her captivity at Tutbury Castle. These represent many hours of painstaking work.

Just outside the grounds of the hall is the partly ruined parish church. Attached to it is a small chantry chapel, where members of the Bedingfield family were buried from the time of Sir Edmund until the late 18th century. The chantry has recently been restored, and has some beautiful early Renaissance terracotta screens.

Oxburgh Hall was once a high-status residence and that can still be appreciated thanks to the careful maintenance of the old building. Restoration work included the manufacture of reproduction rolls of some of the spectacular wallpapers by using surviving scraps of the original wallpaper.

NORWICH CASTLE

LOCATION **NORFOLK, ENGLAND**

DATE BUILT *c.* **1130 (ON SITE OF EARLIER CASTLE)**

FOUNDER **KING HENRY I**

Norwich Castle occupies a lofty position overlooking the city centre, and it has always been a prominent city landmark. The Normans took over the centre of the existing Saxon town, and demolished 96 houses to clear a space for their castle.

The first castle on the site, documented in 1075, was a timber motte and bailey castle. Later, in about 1130, it was rebuilt in stone to make it into a royal palace. The keep and the cathedral were built at about the same time, both of stone brought from Caen in Normandy.

By 1096, Norwich had become so important that the bishopric of East Anglia was moved there. Henry I spent Christmas at Norwich in 1121, and held the symbolic crown-wearing ceremony in the castle. The visit marked Norwich and its castle as the most important royal stronghold in East Anglia.

The gigantic square keep, with three levels, is one of the few to have been built by Henry I. On the highest level is the great hall, with its Victorian balcony. The king's chamber was on a mezzanine floor and had a balcony for the king to look out over the city. The middle level has a false floor which now houses the main museum display and below are interactive displays.

There is a long stone Norman staircase leading up the east wall of the keep to a first-floor entrance in the Bigod Tower. This opens into a large northern chamber, which was the soldiers' hall. The southern half of this floor was subdivided into a knights' chamber, guard room and chapel. Diagonal partitions existed on the west to make a kitchen, pantry and constable's chamber. In the middle was the all-important well.

In 1340, Norwich Castle was handed over to the County Sheriff to become a prison and it became a place of confinement, interrogation, trial and execution. In the wake of the Dissolution, 11 unfortunate conspirators were executed for treason at Norwich Castle in 1537.

In 1834–9 the exterior was refaced and the interior gutted. In 1894, the castle was turned into a museum. It contains many items of interest, like the Snettisham Treasure, a gibbet and death masks.

STOKESAY CASTLE

LOCATION **SHROPSHIRE, ENGLAND**

DATE BUILT *c.* **1240**

FOUNDER **DE SAY FAMILY**

Stokesay Castle is one of the best-preserved fortified manor-houses in England. Late in its history, it was sub-let to farmers who used it for storage and neglected the fabric, but the walls are still in remarkably good condition.

Seen from across the pond on the west side, Stokesay looks complete, but this is an illusion. It is mostly roofless and uninhabitable. The location is remarkable. The castle now stands in a peaceful spot in the hills of south Shropshire. But in the 13th century, which is when Stokesay was built, it was a very dangerous landscape, the Welsh border country, where Marcher lords and their soldiers slept with their swords. Stokesay, meanwhile, had a little moat, which would have been useless against a concerted attack.

The north tower of this toy castle was built in about 1240 by the de Say family. They built their house in a hamlet called South Stoke, which later added the family's name and became Stoke-de-Say. The de Says' choice of location seems to have been an act of faith. They rebuilt the adjacent church.

Laurence de Ludlow, a wealthy wool merchant, bought Stokesay and obtained a licence to crenellate in 1291, from Edward I. It is still not clear whether this was a genuine attempt to turn the manor house into a castle, or a bid for social status. Laurence de Ludlow's family lived at Stokesay for 300 years.

The manor house is built of green-yellow sandstone quarried locally. With its solid-looking tower and crenellated wall, Stokesay looks like a fairytale castle from the south, especially with its half-timbered overhanging storey added to the north tower during Laurence's rebuilding. The south tower has walls of over 2 metres (6 ft) thick, with garderobes built into them. A well near the south tower is 15 metres (50 ft) deep.

The two towers are connected by a banqueting hall, with unusually large pointed windows. The hall was originally aisled, with timber posts. At the southern end of the hall there was a solar accessible by an outside staircase, which was originally roofed, though now open. The solar has two squints, so that ladies in the solar could discreetly observe the goings-on in the hall below.

Many of the original outbuildings have now gone. There was, for instance, a kitchen block, marked now only by its foundations.

Across the courtyard there is a rather incongruous gatehouse, which was added in the 16th century.

Stokesay was clearly never intended to stand up to an organized attack. Cromwell's men laid siege to Stokesay in 1645. The inhabitants wisely surrendered immediately, which meant that minimal damage was done. Only the curtain wall was demolished. This originally rose 9 metres (30 ft) above the moat and was decorated with battlemented parapets; a section remains near the north tower. We must be grateful for the cowardice of the owners; if they had not surrendered quickly, Cromwell's men would probably have pulled down the rest of Stokesay as well.

The Allcroft family, who bought Stokesay in 1896, have taken enormous care to restore and conserve what has survived of one of England's most important domestic ruins.

KENILWORTH CASTLE

LOCATION **WARWICKSHIRE, ENGLAND**

DATE BUILT **1120s**

FOUNDER **CLINTON FAMILY**

The first stone castle at Kenilworth was probably the huge square keep built on the high ground that was earlier occupied by an earth and timber motte and bailey castle.

This was a common pattern with English castles – an early Norman wooden fort, quickly raised to confirm and consolidate William's conquest of England, followed a few decades afterwards by a rebuild in stone.

Work on the stone keep probably began in 1174, when Henry II bought the castle from the Clinton family. Further buildings were added by King John and Henry III. It was Henry III who had the elaborate and original water defences installed; these became a major part of Kenilworth's security. Unfortunately they have now completely gone, but it is known that they involved the damming of several streams to make a very large artificial lake known as 'the mere'. This extended for almost a mile to the west of the castle, and effectively defended it from the west and south. Further pools and moats were made to defend the castle's northern and eastern sides.

Henry III foolishly gave Kenilworth Castle to Simon de Montfort in 1253. Simon, Earl of Leicester, was the king's brother-in-law. By 1256, Simon had taken the leadership of the English barons who opposed the king's weakness and extravagance. Political opposition to the king quickly developed into military opposition, and de Montfort won a spectacular victory over the king at the Battle of Lewes in 1264, capturing both the king and his son, Prince Edward. This victory made Simon a virtual king, but his success was shortlived. Prince Edward managed to escape and gather an army against de Montfort, who was defeated and killed at Evesham in 1265.

De Montfort's son, also called Simon, held Kenilworth, but the following year Henry III and his son, the future Edward I, personally directed their troops in a siege of the castle. Kenilworth held out for several months, thanks mainly to the water defences. Prince Edward mounted an attack over the narrowest of the moats, using wooden siege-towers with catapults on top to hurl boulders at the defenders. He also had barges brought in from Chester, and used these to attack the castle by water – at night. In the end it was shortage of food and an outbreak of fever that made the garrison surrender.

Henry III then granted the castle to his own son, Edmund Earl of Lancaster. In 1361, Kenilworth passed by marriage into the hands of John of Gaunt, who built the opulent Great Hall over a vaulted undercroft on the west side of the keep. With these and ancillary buildings, John of Gaunt made Kenilworth comfortable as well as secure. It was now a palace as well as a castle.

In 1399, the castle became the property of John of Gaunt's son, Henry IV, remaining in the hands of the monarch for a century and a half. Elizabeth I then bestowed Kenilworth Castle on her favourite, Robert Dudley, shortly before she bestowed yet another favour, the Earldom of Leicester. Dudley spent a lot of money – £60,000 – altering the castle and laying out fine gardens with arbours and parterres. He entertained the queen at the improved Kenilworth in lavish style for three weeks in 1575. It is said that Dudley's house-guest and her entourage, which included 31 barons and 400 servants, cost him £1,000 a day – and this was her third visit to Kenilworth. For his queen's entertainment, Dudley laid on music, dancing, hunting and bear-baiting, prize-fighting, pageants, masques and fireworks, to say nothing of the banquets. The queen loved it all. When she arrived, to the sound of trumpets, the clock on the keep, at that time fancifully named 'Caesar's Tower', was dramatically stopped to indicate that time itself stood still for the duration of the queen's visit. To indicate her pleasure at Dudley's hospitality, and to show what a good mood she was in, she knighted Thomas Cecil, the eldest son of Lord Burghley, and four other gentlemen.

On 27 July 1575, the queen rode majestically off to Chartley in Staffordshire, where she expected to be expensively entertained by another of her subjects, Lord Essex. She toured England, bankrupting her loyal subjects. That high summer royal visit was, even so, the high point in Kenilworth's history. When Robert Dudley, Earl of Leicester, died, Kenilworth passed through the hands of several noblemen until the time of the Civil War, when it would suffer the fate of many other English castles.

Cromwell's troops slighted Kenilworth's beautiful sandstone walls and towers, rooted up the magnificent gardens and drained the lake. The local Parliamentarian commander, Major Hawkesworth, converted Leicester's gatehouse into a house for himself. With the Restoration of the monarchy in 1660, the castle fell empty. It was now completely deserted and roofless.

Enough remains of the walls for Kenilworth's grandeur in its heyday to be imagined. John of Gaunt's great hall, 27 metres (90 ft) long, is still very impressive, and well worthy of the King of Castile. Its huge Gothic windows are still there, in the height of 14th-century fashion. So are the fireplaces where the great duke and his third wife, Catherine Swynford, would have warmed themselves. Before the Parliamentarian vandals struck it was described as 'a large and stately hall, of twenty Paces in length, the Roofe whereof is all of Irish wood, neatly and handsomely fram'd. In it is five spacious Chimneys, answerable to soe great a Roome: we next view'd the Great Chamber for the Guard, the Chamber of Presence, the Privy Chamber, fretted above richly with Coats of Armes, and all adorn'd with fayre and rich Chimney Pieces of Alabaster, blacke Marble and of Joyners worke in curious carved wood.'

In the 18th and 19th centuries, Kenilworth was considered a great and picturesque Gothic ruin, completely overgrown. Nathaniel Hawthorne wrote, 'Without the ivy and the shrubbery, this huge Kenilworth would not be a pleasant object.' In the 1930s, work began on clearing the vegetation and debris so that visitors could once more see the third stateliest castle in England. Unfortunately, many of them want to make their own mark on Kenilworth, and the soft sandstone has proved very vulnerable to their scratched graffiti.

The importance of Kenilworth is still evident, just as *The Penny Magazine* described it in 1835:

The annals of this extensive and illustrious fortress are replete with interesting and curious facts, and embrace a great variety of incidents and events calculated to display the national customs and domestic arrangements of our puissant barons, from early epochs of Norman domination in England to the termination of Elizabeth's reign. In contemplating the bold fragments and shattered ruins of this castle, and reflecting on the scenes of warfare and rude pageantry which have prevailed here at different and distant ages, the mind is at once fully occupied and delighted.

WARWICK CASTLE

LOCATION **WARWICKSHIRE, ENGLAND**

DATE BUILT **1068**

FOUNDER **WILLIAM THE CONQUEROR**

Warwick Castle stands on an impressive site, a hill with a steep drop to a river. The site was chosen by William the Conqueror, according to Ordericus Vitalis, and a castle was built there in 1068.

William was determined to subdue the northern Saxon lords, and to do this he needed to create a network of strongholds. Warwick had a high mound surmounted by a shell-keep, and fragments of this can still be seen. On the south side its bailey was defended by the river cliff and the River Avon. The other sides were defended by a wide, deep moat.

The Saxon King Alfred began the systematic refortification of England, but the bulk of the actual work was done by his successors in the early tenth century, Edward the Elder and Aethelflaed, the Lady of Mercia. It was Aethelflaed who built the fortified town of Warwick, and there may well have been a Saxon timber fort on the site of the stone castle we see today.

Warwick was a typical medieval castle, with ad hoc alterations going on virtually continuously. It was always held by the monarch or a powerful subject, so it always had a high political and military profile. In the Barons' War, Simon de Montfort attacked and damaged the defences; the Beauchamps took the castle over shortly after this and remained its owners for 200 years.

Warwick Castle was given an expensive face-lift at the end of the 14th century by the rich and powerful Beauchamp family. Lavish and spacious living quarters were built in a massive range against the curtain wall overlooking the river. There were washing sinks fitted with drains even in the servants' quarters. Medieval manners placed great emphasis on keeping hands clean, largely because people ate with their fingers.

The 'bastard feudal' style was in fashion. At Warwick, the Beauchamps built two big corner towers in the curtain wall symmetrically on each side of the gatehouse. Each contained several storeys of well-appointed and well-lit chambers with fireplaces, garderobes and bedchambers fitted into the thickness of the walls. Caesar's Tower is a beautiful development of a round

LEFT The grounds of Warwick Castle were landscaped by Capability Brown and over the years the estate and residence were tranformed into a grand stately home.

RIGHT The polygonal Guy's Tower.

tower, a three-lobed tower, which looks like three round towers coalescing. It stands an imposing 41 metres (133 ft) high from the base of its massive plinth near the river bank. Each of its storeys has stone vaulting except the top one, making the tower as a whole fireproof. The lowest storey was a prison. Since the big round tower was known in France as a 'donjon', such prisons became 'dungeons'. On the top were two tiers of ingeniously designed battlements. The second tier is like a second, slightly smaller, tower standing on top of the larger one. Guy's Tower is similar in size, but polygonal and lacking the dungeon. The placing of the two giant towers implies an eagerness to impress, and they had a lot more to do with social status than military necessity.

Warwick Castle became a major seat of power in the middle ages, especially when Richard Neville, Earl of Warwick, was its owner. It was this Warwick who played a major part in putting Edward IV on the throne, and so became 'Warwick the King-maker'.

The earldom changed hands several times until in 1604 James I presented it – and the now-dilapidated castle – to Sir Fulke Greville. Warwick Castle remained in the hands of the Greville family until 1978. According to the epitaph he chose for himself, Fulke Greville was 'Servant of Queen Elizabeth, Counsellor to King James, Friend to Sir Philip Sidney'. He was a poet and his writings, mostly unpublished in his lifetime, show him to be a shrewd observer and moralist. He probably first attended Elizabeth I's court in Sir Philip Sidney's company in 1575. He was friendly with the Earl of Essex, yet somehow escaped retribution when Essex

was beheaded for treason in 1601. He continued in favour with both Elizabeth and James I. He became Chancellor of the Exchequer in 1614. In 1617, James I visited him at Warwick Castle. After James I died in 1625, Fulke Greville attended Charles I's court. In 1628 he was stabbed to death by his servant, Ralph Haywood, who was angry at what he considered the ungenerous legacy Sir Fulke left to him in his will.

The castle was bought by the Tussaud's Group in 1978 and extensively restored. The state rooms have been enhanced with some imaginative and incredibly lifelike waxworks. One shows an Edwardian soiree, with a bearded gentleman in evening dress playing the piano, accompanying a young lady singing. The state dining room dates from 1763, when it was commissioned by Francis Greville. The great hall is the largest room in the castle. With its carpets and fine furniture, it looks far more opulent and comfortable today than it would have looked in earlier days. Instead of carpets, there would have been rushes. The room would have been smoky and the atmosphere dark and strong-smelling. The castle chapel is a small but beautiful building, erected in the early 1600s; it is thought that an earlier chapel stood on the same spot.

Warwick has many of its rooms on show, including drawing rooms, bedrooms, music room, library and smoking room. The building itself is an inspiring evocation of the medieval past, and there are many events and attractions that are of interest.

ELY CATHEDRAL

LOCATION **CAMBRIDGESHIRE, ENGLAND**
DATE BUILT **1083 (ON SITE OF EARLIER ABBEY)**
FOUNDER **ABBOT SIMEON**

The city of Ely may be tiny, but its cathedral is huge. At 158 metres (517 ft), it is one of the longest churches in England. It is also one of the most varied architecturally.

The name 'Ely' means 'Eel Island', and the city stands on a low, dry island of gravel about 21 metres (70 ft) above the reclaimed marshland. Although this is not high, it is high enough to make the huge cathedral very conspicuous in the vast plain of the Fens.

The first building at Ely was a Benedictine abbey for monks and nuns, founded by St Etheldreda, Queen of Northumbria. She settled at this secluded island in the Fens when she retired from the world in 673 to become Ely's first abbess. After her death in 679 miracles were reported by those praying at her shrine, and Ely became a major focus for Saxon pilgrims.

In 870 the Danes sacked the abbey, but it was refounded a few decades later by King Edgar (959–75) as a Benedictine monastery. Following the Norman invasion, Ely was used as a headquarters by the Saxon resistance led by Hereward the Wake in 1070–1.

William I appointed a fellow Norman, Simeon, as abbot, and Simeon began work on the present structure in 1083. The Norman transepts and east end were finished in 1106. In 1109 the church was raised to cathedral status, though the Norman nave was not completed until 1189. The nave is narrow, almost 76 metres (250 ft) long and made up of 12 bays. It is an imposing piece of late Norman architecture, virtually contemporary with the nave of Peterborough cathedral. The piers are fairly massive, as Norman pillars usually are, but lighter than those of Durham or Gloucester. The original plain roof has been replaced by a 19th-century ceiling, which some people may like.

In the south aisle of the nave is the prior's doorway, which was built in about 1140. This is normally kept locked in winter, but on the outside it has a richly carved tympanum, the semicircular panel contained between the door lintel and the arch. This tympanum shows Christ in majesty, and such

The Norman nave of 12 bays was finished in 1189. It now has a highly decorated 19th-century ceiling.

compositions are sometimes just called 'Majesties'. The pilasters are also carved, with figures of beasts and men.

Close to this door is the plinth of a Saxon cross, which is called Ovin's Stone. It was dedicated to Ovinus, a leading Anglo-Saxon in the time of Queen Etheldreda.

Near the west end of the nave is the grave of Alan de Walsingham, the architect of the octagon. His brass has unfortunately gone.

The transepts are large. They are also unusual in having aisles, just like miniature naves. The lower walls of the transepts have some of the oldest surviving masonry in the cathedral, dating from as early as 1083.

The choir contains the tomb of John Tiptoft, Earl of Worcester, between his two wives; he was beheaded in 1470 during the Wars of the Roses. In front of the high altar there is an inscribed slate slab marking the site of the shrine of St Etheldreda.

The Galilee, or west porch, was added in about 1200. Bishop Hugh of Northwold lengthened the choir by six graceful bays in the Early English style, and these were the setting for St Etheldreda's shrine.

In 1322, disaster struck. The central tower fell down, wrecking the Norman nave. This gave the sacrist Alan de Walsingham and his team of craftsmen an opportunity to try something new. They designed the beautiful and entirely original octagonal lantern above the crossing – a much lighter and therefore safer structure than the Norman stone tower.

The chantry chapels at the east end of the church were built later in the Perpendicular style, between 1490 and 1520. The unsatisfactory and asymmetrical appearance of the west front is simply explained by the collapse of the north-west tower in 1701. The west front is full of interest, but badly needs restoration to its original symmetry.

Ultimately, it is the unique central octagon that is the cathedral's main interest – and one of the marvels of medieval architecture. The timber lantern was restored by Sir George Gilbert Scott in the 19th century. When viewed from below, the interlaced timberwork is as fascinating to look at as the stone tracery of a decorated window. Aesthetically the octagon works well, supplying an oasis of light and airy space in the midst of some rather heavy and oppressive Norman stonework. It has been compared to a huge starfish, with the light-filled space of the lantern as the body and the vaulting that spreads the weight out to the supporting columns as the arms. The wooden lantern weighs 400 tons, and the engineers had to search far and wide throughout England to find oaks big enough for the corner posts, which are 19 metres (63 ft) long. The master carpenter employed by Alan de Walsingham was William Hurley, the most famous carpenter of his day.

High up on the arches of the octagon are carved stone heads, including portraits of Edward

Ely Cathedral is a majestic example of late Norman architecture, its tower visible for miles across the flat Cambridgeshire Fens.

III, Queen Philippa, Alan de Walsingham, Prior Crauden and Bishop Hotham, though these can only be appreciated with binoculars. A tour round the outside of Ely Cathedral offers a constantly changing kaleidoscope of shapes and surfaces, from the bluff straightforwardness of the Norman work to the ornate and fancy work of the octagon. The octagonal top storey of the tower is decorated in style, but the lower part belongs to the late Norman period.

The west front is odd. Normally west fronts have a flanking tower on each side. Ely was designed to have flanking towers, but the north-west tower fell down in a storm in 1701 and was never rebuilt. The effect of the complete design could be impressive, but the continuing lopsidedness is entirely unsatisfactory.

From a distance, Ely Cathedral can look far less appealing, rising forbiddingly from the flat Fens like a beached oil tanker.

FRAMLINGHAM CASTLE

LOCATION **SUFFOLK, ENGLAND**
DATE BUILT **1101**
FOUNDER **ROGER BIGOD**

Framlingham is one of the most beautiful medieval castles in Britain. The site was probably fortified in the Saxon period.

An early Norman timber castle was raised there in the 11th century. Roger Bigod is the first known owner of the castle, and he was granted Framlingham in 1101 by Henry I. Bigod's second son, Hugh, inherited Framlingham, became Earl of Norfolk and probably built a motte type of castle in *c.* 1140.

Hugh later quarrelled with Henry II and in retaliation the king confiscated Framlingham. In 1165, Hugh raised enough money to buy his castle back, but he was implicated in the barons' revolt in 1173 and the castle was once again confiscated – and this time completely destroyed.

When Richard I came to the throne, Hugh's son Roger regained ownership of Framlingham. It was Roger who built the castle as we now see it, with its splendid polygonal curtain wall laced with 13 graceful towers. It was a revolutionary design that enabled a large force of infantry and cavalry to be housed and protected.

The castle changed hands several times. The Dukes of Norfolk made it their chief residence in the 15th century. The second duke modernized the castle, using brick extensively, adding the fine bridge and gatehouse, and topping the towers with a set of magnificent Tudor chimneys – most purely for decorative effect. Unusually, Framlingham does not have a keep. A larger outer bailey formerly existed to the east and south and in the 16th century enclosed most of the town. It was huge, and could house an entire army.

Henry VIII confiscated Framlingham; later Edward VI gave it to his half-sister, Mary Tudor. For a moment it stood at the centre of British history. When Edward VI died in 1553, Mary was challenged by the Duke of Northumberland in support of his daughter-in-law, Lady Jane Grey. Mary retreated to her castle at Framlingham before her final triumph.

ORFORD CASTLE

LOCATION **SUFFOLK, ENGLAND**
DATE BUILT **1160s**
FOUNDER **KING HENRY II**

Orford Castle stands close to the bleak, windswept coast of Suffolk, on the River Alde. It overlooks Orford, which was a busy, thriving port in medieval times.

Orford is one of Henry II's castles, built at huge expense in the 1160s. It was intended to assert the king's authority over East Anglia and challenge the power of the Earl of Norfolk. Henry encouraged his designer, Maurice the Engineer, to move away from the standard keep design – a cube with a tower at each corner – towards a circular plan by way of a polygon. The tower is a remarkable 21-sided shape, probably inspired by European designs. Orford stands complete, a kind of freak, a prototype of the truly cylindrical keeps that would be built in the 13th century.

Orford Castle, its walls built of cheap local flint and expensively imported Caen stone from Normandy, was habitable by the year 1168. By 1170, the keep was fitted with an innovative curtain wall with rectangular towers, though this has now gone. All we are left with is the astonishing polygonal keep built in 1165–7. It has three squarish angle-towers, like the conventional cube shape, but they huddle round a compressed polygonal core. The circular interior contains many rooms over five floors, including kitchens and a chapel. From the tower there is a fine view across Orford Ness.

Towering polygonal keeps like this turned out to be transitional. In succeeding decades, the traditional cube-shaped keeps went on being built, and the polygonal keep evolved into a strong new type, the big round keep. But Orford Castle was an important step in the development of Henry II's ideas on castle-building. In the 33 years of Henry's reign, about £21,000 was spent on castles. Of that sum, around two-thirds went on minor repairs and modifications – and of course maintenance.

After King John's death, the castle was taken by the French claimant to the throne, Prince Louis. Orford was to change hands several times subsequently, but the fine stonework of Maurice's castle remains virtually intact; it has not been involved in any military action, and that has saved it.

HEDINGHAM CASTLE

LOCATION **ESSEX, ENGLAND**

DATE BUILT **1130**

FOUNDER **AUBREY DE VERE**

Hedingham Castle is dominated by its great four-storey square keep. It boasts what is considered to be one of the best surviving – and best-preserved – examples of Norman military towers.

The keep was built in about 1130 by Aubrey de Vere, within a bailey surrounded by a moat. It is a very imposing piece of architecture and unusually tall. When complete it stood over 30 metres (100 ft) high, with walls 3.6 metres (12 ft) thick at the base. The walls are of rubble faced with neatly coursed Barnack stone, most of which is still in place.

The entrance to the keep was by way of an exterior staircase to a door at first-floor level. The doorway has a fine carved Romanesque arch with zigzag ornament and round attached columns on each side. Inside, there was a spiral staircase rising to the battlements, where the four angle turrets and a protective parapet rose above roof level. The staircase was mounted in a clockwise direction to enable retreating defenders to use their sword arms effectively, but with little room for attackers to swing their swords.

The keep was fitted with wall fireplaces, and was one of the earliest English castles to have chimney flues built into the walls. The de Vere family were clearly interested in domestic comfort as well as military strength. The hall on the second floor was a splendid chamber, with a gallery all the way round it and a huge round arch supporting the lofty ceiling.

The de Vere family supported the House of Lancaster in the Wars of the Roses, and died as a result. These sacrifices were not rewarded by the Tudor monarchs. When John de Vere entertained Henry VII here, he went to a lot of expense, and assembled a large retinue of retainers in his Oxford livery. His Majesty was daunted by what he evidently saw as a show of strength and chillingly pointed out that de Vere had broken a law forbidding this practice.

The ruinous state of Hedingham today is, unusually, not due to the Civil War but to the folly of one of its owners, the 17th Earl of Oxford: he dismantled it at the end of the 16th century and left it in its current state.

BERKHAMSTED CASTLE

LOCATION **HERTFORDSHIRE, ENGLAND**

DATE BUILT **11TH CENTURY**

FOUNDER **ROBERT DE MORTAIN**

Berkhamsted Castle is a classic example of a Norman motte and bailey originally of timber and later rebuilt in stone. There is a large bailey with fragments of its curtain wall still standing and a large artificial mound, or motte, to one side.

There are traces on top of the motte of the foundations of a round stone tower with a rectangular fore-building. The bailey has two wards, with a small inner ward below the motte and the west tower in the large outer ward.

The most extraordinary feature is the complicated defensive work on the outside of the bailey, where there are two moats separated by a huge earthen rampart. Berkhamsted Castle was built in the late 11th century at the orders of Robert de Mortain, who was William the Conqueror's half-brother.

A hundred years after Robert's timber fort was built, Henry II's chancellor and archbishop, Thomas Becket, became its owner. During Becket's time, following the civil war in the reign of King Stephen, the wooden palisades round the motte and bailey were replaced with stone walls. In the reign of King John further defences were added, including wing walls up the slope of the motte and round towers along the bailey curtain wall. These extra defences were put to the test in 1216, when Prince Louis of France laid siege to the castle during an attempt to seize John's crown. The castle fell after an onslaught from giant catapults called mangonels; this attack lasted two weeks.

Later owners of Berkhamsted included Richard Duke of Cornwall, who probably built the three-storey tower on the western section of the curtain wall. Edward the Black Prince was another owner.

Berkhamsted fell into disuse in 1495 and was never occupied after that. The final indignity came in 1838, when the barbican with its gatehouse was demolished to make way for the London and Birmingham Railway.

Archaeologists have examined the earthworks and concluded that they were built for King John in the weeks immediately before the 1216 siege.

DONNINGTON CASTLE

LOCATION **WEST BERKSHIRE, ENGLAND**

DATE BUILT **1386**

FOUNDER **SIR RICHARD ABBERBURY**

Donnington Castle is a classic ruin of great beauty, which speaks eloquently of the medieval spirit and the savagery of the Civil War. It stands on a hilltop overlooking the River Lambourne, about a mile north of Newbury.

The castle was the home of Sir Richard Abberbury, who acquired a licence to crenellate his property in 1386. Although it had no moat, Donnington Castle turned out to be one of the most formidable castles ever built in England.

The castle was a rectangular enclosure with a massive round tower at each corner and two square towers or turrets midway along the two longest sides. The curtain wall enclosed the domestic building arranged round a courtyard. The most impressive part of the castle, and the only part still standing, was the gatehouse. This three-storey rectangular building has two lofty round towers flanking the entrance. One has red-brick repairs where a large hole was blasted out by a Parliamentarian mortar in the Civil War.

Abberbury sold Donnington to Thomas, Geoffrey Chaucer's son, but he in turn sold it to Sir John Phelipp, his son-in-law. Princess Elizabeth later owned the castle, and spent some time there in fearful retirement while her dangerous half-sister Mary Tudor was on the throne.

Donnington Castle was seized by Royalist forces during the Civil War following the Battle of Newbury. Earthworks were raised round the castle in the form of a star, which successfully withstood a Parliamentary siege in 1644. Charles I took an army to relieve Donnington Castle and the second Battle of Newbury was fought round it.

The second siege continued for 18 months. Terms were finally agreed for a conditional surrender, but only after heavy bombardment had reduced the castle to an almost total ruin. The 200-strong garrison were allowed to march out of the castle unimpeded and rejoin the Royalist army at Wallingford. The earthworks raised in the Civil War can still be seen round the castle.

WINDSOR CASTLE

LOCATION **WINDSOR & MAIDENHEAD, ENGLAND**

DATE BUILT **1070s**

FOUNDER **WILLIAM THE CONQUEROR**

Windsor is the largest inhabited castle in the world, and the oldest in continuous occupation; English kings and queens have lived there for 900 years.

Windsor Castle, proclaimed by Pepys in the 17th century to be 'the most romantique castle that is in the world', had its beginnings a thousand years earlier, when the Saxons settled at Clewer. There may well have been a late Saxon fort on the site of the castle, but the first record we have is of the fort built immediately after the Norman Conquest in 1066. The manor, aptly, belonged to King Harold himself, and he had a palace at Old Windsor; William gave most of the manor away, but kept half a hide bearing an ancient earthwork for himself, and it was here he built his castle, probably in stone from the start; the mound on which the keep stands is a natural chalk hill, and therefore capable of bearing immense weights of stone masonry.

Windsor had obvious strategic significance, overlooking and commanding the middle Thames.

The shell-keep at Windsor is an outstanding building. Following William I's construction, the keep was remodelled by Henry II and Edward III and finally reshaped in the 19th century. In 1820, it was refaced with new stone and doubled to its present height of 19.5 metres (64 ft). The keep's walls contain a bewildering mix of stonework dating from the 11th, 12th, 14th and 19th centuries.

Windsor quickly became a favourite royal palace, third in rank behind the Tower and Winchester. William II held a council at Windsor, imprisoning the rebel Earl of Mowbray there for the remaining 30 years of his life. Henry II often stayed at Windsor, and had the outer stone curtain wall built in 1175 so that more troops could be garrisoned there.

258

St George's Chapel was begun in 1475 and is a fine example of late-medieval architecture.

Henry III did much to improve Windsor. The old hall in the upper ward was abandoned in favour of a new and larger one in the lower ward. In 1272, he roofed the keep. On the town side of the castle, he built three great towers. On the north, he raised another tower on the site now occupied by the Winchester Tower. All the buildings were finely decorated and the windows fitted with glass, which was then a new luxury.

In 1312, Edward III was born at Windsor. During this king's long reign there were many scenes of pomp and ceremony at Windsor, with feasts, processions, tournaments and great assemblies. King Edward was guiding his royal prisoners, King John of France and King David of Scotland, round the lower ward one day when one of them rashly pointed out that the upper ward lay on higher ground and would command a finer view. King Edward agreed and added pleasantly that he would indeed move his castle accordingly and that their two ransoms would cover the cost of the work.

King Edward III was fired by the idea of King Arthur and the Round Table. He wanted to found an order of Knights of the Round Table, and got his carpenters and masons busy with the task of creating a special building to accommodate a round banqueting table. The building was based on the timber lantern at Ely Cathedral; it has completely vanished. The table, made of 52 oaks, seems to have been in the shape of a horseshoe, to allow servants to serve the food and drink. The new order of chivalry became the Order of the Garter.

Prince James of Scotland was held prisoner here for many years. It was while in relaxed captivity that he wrote 'The King's Quair' about his love for the king's niece, Jane Beaufort, whom he eventually married. Ironically, these years were probably the happiest of the young prince's life. When he was released to become King of Scots it was to a gloomy reign culminating in assassination by his own nobles in 1437.

Edward IV was the first English monarch to be buried at Windsor. His treacherous brother, the Duke of Clarence, had been executed in the Tower on Edward's orders and then buried at Windsor. In 1484, the remains of the murdered Henry VI were transferred from Chertsey Abbey on the orders of Richard III – and buried beside those of his arch-rival, Edward IV. In 1789, some workmen came across the lead coffin of Edward IV. When it was opened, the skeleton was found to be 1.9 metres (6ft 4in) tall. A lock of the king's hair was taken from the coffin and deposited in the Ashmolean Museum in Oxford.

Queen Elizabeth was very fond of Windsor, sometimes staying there the whole of the autumn and Christmas. One of the queen's favourite characters in Shakespeare was Sir John Falstaff, and she expressed a desire to see 'Falstaff in love'; Shakespeare obligingly wrote *The Merry Wives of Windsor* to please her twice over.

The 1992 fire, on Elizabeth II's wedding anniversary, damaged or destroyed over a hundred rooms. The restoration took five years and £37,000,000 to complete. The disaster prompted searching questions about responsibility for the building and its repair; is Windsor Castle owned by the monarch or the state?

The magnificent St George's Chapel, begun in 1475 by Edward IV and completed by Henry VIII, is one of the finest examples of late-medieval architecture in England. Ten monarchs are buried in the chapel, including Henry VIII, who lies with Jane Seymour.

The state apartments are lavishly decorated formal rooms that are still in use for state functions and receptions; they form the centre of a working palace, though they are also open to the public. There is also an outstanding art collection, including works by Leonardo, Rembrandt, Rubens and Van Dyck, and a large collection of armour.

The gloriously souped-up medieval extravaganza that we see today at Windsor is still fundamentally Edward III's castle, but heavily restored. Some 650 years ago, King Edward spent an incredible £50,000 on Windsor, by far the largest sum any sovereign spent on any single building in the entire middle ages. It was possible only because of Edward's vision, compulsion and sheer ruthlessness. But then, what else is a castle if not a display of brute power?

WESTMINSTER ABBEY

LOCATION **GREATER LONDON, ENGLAND**

DATE BUILT **1065**

FOUNDER **KING EDWARD THE CONFESSOR**

Westminster Abbey occupies a unique place in English history; it is both the crowning place and the burial place of most English monarchs. Despite this, Westminster began unpromisingly, as a gravel island in the middle of the marshy floodplain of the Thames.

The first church of which there is any record is the Benedictine abbey dedicated to St Peter in the tenth century. This was the monastery, the 'West Minster', that Edward the Confessor took over and rebuilt on a grander scale. His Romanesque church was consecrated in 1065. The king died a year later and was buried in it. In this church, every single monarch since Harold has been crowned, except for Edward V and Edward VIII, who went uncrowned.

Most of the present structure of the abbey is in the Early English style, with the major exceptions of Henry VII's magnificent chapel at the east end, which is in Perpendicular style, and the towers on the west front, which were rebuilt in the 18th century. In 1220 a Lady Chapel was added at the east end. In 1245 Henry III decided he would honour Edward the Confessor by rebuilding the entire church in a more magnificent style, and it is that abbey church that we see today. It was consecrated in 1269. From then on, it became customary for monarchs to be buried in the abbey church.

Both exterior and interior have been rebuilt over the years, but some Norman work still survives in the Chamber of the Pyx and its undercroft. Wren and Wyatt did restoration work in 1697–1720. The two west towers were designed by Nicholas Hawksmoor in 1735.

It has the tallest Gothic nave in England. Above the arcades is a double triforium with lavish tracery, and above that the tall clerestory. The nave is full of post-Reformation monuments and memorials to people in public life. It also includes the tomb of the Unknown Soldier.

The Chapel of Henry VII has superb fan vaulting and graceful windows. The shrine of Edward the Confessor still retains its original 13th-century stonework in its lower storey. Nearby is the Coronation Chair, an oak throne made in 1300.

ENTRY TO THE TRAITORS' GATE

TOWER OF LONDON

LOCATION GREATER LONDON, ENGLAND
DATE BUILT BETWEEN 1066–71
FOUNDER WILLIAM THE CONQUEROR

Most of the first-generation castles built after the Norman Conquest were made of timber; only later was stone used. The Tower of London, however, was special – it was built in stone from the start.

The Romans decided that the river crossing was important enough to defend with a fort and then an enclosing wall, which eventually became the wall of the City of London. The city then needed to be defended against possible invasion from the sea, which meant building a fortress at the point where the seaward end of the city wall reached the Thames. This was where William the Conqueror built his greatest castle.

The site may have an even longer ancestry. Tradition says that Julius Caesar was the founder of the Tower, and archaeologists have partly verified this by finding traces of Roman fortifications under the medieval walls.

In the years immediately after Hastings, William's aim was to build as many small timber motte-and-bailey castles as he could defend, mostly overlooking towns. Between 1066 and 1071, castles sprang up at Lincoln, Chester, Stafford, Tutbury, Shrewsbury, Wisbech, Norwich, Huntingdon, Worcester, Clifford, Hereford, Ewyas Harold, Cambridge, Oxford, Monmouth, Pevensey, Winchester, Dover, Hastings, York – and London. The Domesday Book of 1086-7 mentions 49 castles as existing at that time. Of the 49 listed, 33 were standing on sites that had already been fortified before 1066. This means that many of the castles credited to William the Conqueror were remodelled Saxon or even older castles. Portchester Castle has a square Norman keep in the corner of a square Roman fort. At Pevensey, a square Norman keep stands rather oddly within an elliptical Roman curtain wall.

The magnificent White Tower at the Tower of London was the very finest of these great square keeps. It was built of ragstone rubble with ashlar dressings, walls between 3.7 metres (12 ft) and 4.6 metres (15 ft) feet thick at the base and 27 metres (90 ft) high – the corner turrets rising even higher. There were also projections formed by the end of the chapel and the staircase.

The White Tower is a world-famous example of a massive square Norman keep. In recent years it has been the subject of a huge conservation project designed to protect its important fabric.

William Rufus added an inner bailey between the White Tower and the Thames. This was later destroyed. A middle bailey was created in 1190 and a Bell Tower in the Plantagenet period. In 1300 Edward I completed the outer bailey, the moat, three outer gates and a barbican. Throughout all these changes and later developments, the core of the castle remained the imposing keep designed by Gundulf, the talented Bishop of Rochester, and completed in 1078.

The curtain wall of the Tower encloses a large irregular hexagon, which is surrounded by a substantial moat which is now dry, though there are plans to flood it again. Two lines of fortifications enclose the inner bailey, where the White Tower stands. The walls of the White Tower were restored by Christopher Wren, but in Norman style, and all is Norman within.

Among the surrounding buildings are a 19th-century barracks – the Tower was still garrisoned until modern times – and the Chapel of St Peter ad Vincula, which

was built in the 12th century but remodelled in the 14th and 16th centuries.

The Ballium Wall is the inner of the two lines of fortification and dates from the same time as the keep. Studding the Ballium Wall at intervals are 13 towers. One is the Wakefield Tower, where for a long time the crown jewels were kept and displayed. This was also the oratory where the deposed Henry VI was kept prisoner and also where he was killed, in 1471, on the orders of Edward IV.

The main entrance to the Tower is through the Middle Tower in the west. Beside it there was a menagerie or zoo from Norman times right through to the 19th century. Access is by way of a bridge over the moat and then through the Byward Tower.

On the south, giving entry to the Tower from the river through St Thomas's Tower and the Bloody Tower, is the famous Traitor's Gate. Prisoners of rank were usually conducted to the Tower by river rather than through the streets of London, and they were delivered to the steps under the menacing low arch of this gate. It is not open to the river any longer because of the increasing risk of tidal flooding; an embankment bars access today. The great interest the Tower of London holds for us today is its connection over several centuries with distinguished prisoners and their fateful executions, often by public beheading, sometimes by secret assassination.

The Beauchamp Tower was for a long time the main place of confinement for high-ranking prisoners, but there are chambers and dungeons all over the Tower complex that are associated with one prisoner or another. The Bell Tower accommodated Princess Elizabeth, Bishop Fisher and Sir Thomas More. The Bowyer Tower was the prison of the Duke of Clarence, the treacherous brother of Edward IV and Richard III. Shakespeare portrayed Richard III as Clarence's murderer, but it was Edward IV who had Clarence executed, and it was Clarence himself who asked to die by being ducked head-first into a butt of Malmsey.

The Salt Tower and the Broad Arrow Tower were the places where the Catholic prisoners of Queen Elizabeth I's reign were incarcerated. The Martin Tower was where Colonel Blood carried out his almost-successful attempt to steal the crown jewels, which at that time were kept there.

Executions were carried out both within the Tower and very publicly on Tower Hill. An area marked out on Tower Green is shown to tourists as the site of the block, but the scaffold was normally erected in the open space to the south of the White Tower. Many of those executed were buried in the Chapel of St Peter ad Vincula, such as Sir Thomas More, Queen Anne Boleyn, Queen Katharine Howard, Lady Jane Grey and the Duke of Monmouth.

The association of the Tower with high-profile prisoners such as Sir Walter Raleigh tends to put a heavy emphasis on the Tower as a prison. It certainly continued to be a prison through the 19th century, and was even used occasionally as a military prison in the 20th century. The last prisoners were the Kray twins, who were imprisoned there briefly following their arrest as army deserters.

The Tower was not just a prison and a fortress, though. It was a royal palace, from at least the reign of King Stephen until the time of Oliver Cromwell. The Tower continues to be a fortress of sorts, policed by Yeomen Warders, known as 'Beefeaters', who wear Tudor uniforms.

Because of the part it has played in so many significant episodes of English history, the Tower has become a potent symbol of English history. To understand fully all the things that have happened within its still-forbidding walls is to understand the history of England itself.

ROCHESTER CASTLE

LOCATION MEDWAY, ENGLAND

DATE BUILT 1088/1127

FOUNDER WILLIAM RUFUS/WILLIAM OF CORBEUIL

Rochester's Norman keep is an uncompromisingly aggressive building – raw, externally undecorated, and as rough as a sea-cliff.

It was in 1088 that William Rufus persuaded Gundulf to build a high stone curtain wall round the bailey at Rochester, to make the wooden keep more secure. It guarded Rochester and the important Medway river crossing on the London–Dover road, a key strategic site that had been fortified in Roman times. In 1125, Henry I entrusted Archbishop William of Corbeuil with Rochester Castle and gave him permission to rebuild in stone.

What the archbishop built was indeed 'an outstanding tower'. When complete, 13 years later, it rose through five floors to a height of 38 metres (125 ft), making it the tallest keep in England. It was built with walls 3.7 metres (12 ft) thick made of Kentish ragstone and Caen stone facings. It was intended to be an imposing, even menacing, building. It still is today.

A forebuilding gave external access to the keep at first floor level. A partition wall divided the keep into two equal halves. This wall was pierced by round arches decorated with carved chevrons and supported by thin round columns. There was a well-shaft running right up through the building, so that water was available on every floor, and also a stone newel staircase.

In 1215, in the reign of King John, Rochester Castle withstood a ferocious three-month siege. The defenders were able to continue fighting even after John's soldiers had broken into the tower, surrendering only after they ran out of food. According to a contemporary chronicler, when this most impregnable of fortresses fell, 'men no longer put their trust in castles'. Rochester was the peak of development of the great square keep.

During the Hundred Years War, Rochester, though now very out of date, was refortified, with an eye on a possible attack by the French on the Thames estuary. By 1561 the grand old tower-keep was a relic from a bygone age. Stone from the old Norman curtain wall was taken to build a new castle at Upnor, opposite the naval base at Chatham.

LEEDS CASTLE

LOCATION **KENT, ENGLAND**

DATE BUILT **857**

FOUNDER **LEDIAN, CHIEF MINISTER OF ETHELBERT IV**

Like Bodiam, Leeds Castle is a fairytale castle that seems to float on a great lake. It was built in 857 by Ledian, the chief minister of Ethelbert IV, King of Kent, who saw the lake formed by the River Len, with the two islands in the middle, as a perfect site for his castle.

Ledian built a wooden fort on the two islands. Ethelbert, it was said, 'governed with love and honour'; one of its more recent owners said that Leeds Castle was always 'a happy castle'.

In common with many Anglo-Saxon castles, it has been forgotten, but the Norman invaders quickly recognized the value of the site. William I gave Leeds to his half-brother, Bishop Odo of Bayeux. When Odo rebelled, William took the castle back and granted it to Hamon de Crevecour, who had fought with the king at Hastings. De Crevecour started building the stone castle in the reign of Henry I, in 1119. The family was very pious, perhaps because of a curse that hung over them.

For over 200 years the castle stayed in the de Crevecour family. Hamon, the great-grandson of Robert de Crevecour, was one of the rebel barons in the reign of King John. In the reign of Henry III he became Warden of the Cinque Ports. His son Robert fought against Henry III and when the king decisively won the Battle of Evesham the family fortunes went into a steep decline. The de Crevecours were forced to give up Leeds Castle, which the king granted to one of his devoted supporters, Sir Roger de Leyburn. Both Roger and his son William were great soldiers and loyal to the crown; William gave his castle to Edward I in 1278.

Edward I and his queen loved Leeds Castle, using it much as the present royal family uses Balmoral. The king spent a lot of money extending the castle. Until this time, the defence of the castle depended mainly on the lake. On the islands themselves, there was little in the way of defensive work. Edward I decided that this was unsatisfactory

and added a high-bastioned outer wall to make an outer bailey, a barbican and the gloriette, a D-shaped tower functioning as a mini-fortress on the smaller island. The new walls rose straight out of the water. The gatehouse was also enlarged.

Edward I, unusually, loved his wife, Eleanor of Castile – it was not a mere dynastic marriage – and gave the perfected Leeds Castle to her as a present. He routinely addressed Eleanor, in French, as 'chère reine', 'dear queen'. The cross he raised in London to her on her death was known as 'Chère Reine Croix', which has become Charing Cross. When the king remarried, he gave Leeds Castle to his second wife, Margaret. This association led to Leeds being nicknamed the Ladies' Castle.

Edward II granted Leeds Castle to Lord Badlesmere. When Queen Isabella called to stay

the night in the summer of 1321, she was testing Badlesmere's loyalty. Walter Culpeper was constable of the castle. He was bold enough to refuse Queen Isabella entry to the castle, advising her to 'seek some other lodging'. 'The Captain most malapertly repulsed her, insomuch that she complained grievously to the King', Edward II, who laid siege to the castle in the November, used ballistas or springalds and an army of 30,000 men to force a surrender. 'Then he tooke Captaine Colepeper and hoong him up'. Lord Badlesmere was sent to the Tower and later beheaded. In 1327, Queen Isabella took the castle for herself, and kept it until her death in 1358.

Edward III carried out many repairs. The chambers of the king and queen in the gloriette were improved and a new garderobe especially for the king was installed.

In 1395, the French historian Froissart met Richard II at Leeds Castle; Froissart mentions it in his Chronicles. 'I shewd not the kynge the boke that I hadde brought for hym, he was so sore occupyed with great affayres.' At this time, the clerk of works at Leeds Castle was none other than Henry Yevele, the great architect who was responsible for the roof of Westminster Hall and the astonishingly beautiful nave at Canterbury Cathedral, the finest piece of medieval architecture in England.

Henry IV, who took Richard's throne, gave Leeds to his wife, Queen Joan of Navarre. They spent the summer of 1403 there to avoid the plague in London. In 1412, Joan gave the castle to Thomas Arundel, Archbishop of Canterbury. It was to Leeds Castle that the Archbishop summoned Sir John Oldcastle to stand trial for heresy.

The sixth and last queen to receive Leeds as a dower from her husband was Catherine de Valois, Henry V's queen. She acquired it in 1423, installing a clock and bell in 1435. The bell was last rung on the present queen's visit to Leeds Castle in 1985. When

Henry V died, Catherine was still only 21. She fell in love with Owen Tudor, the Welshman who was Clerk of the Queen's Wardrobe, looking after her dresses and jewels. Leeds Castle seems a perfect setting for this remarkable romance between the 'dowager' queen and her servant. When their affair was discovered they were imprisoned, but Owen Tudor escaped and Catherine was released. They had, however, been secretly married. Their son, Edmund, became the father of Henry VII.

Henry VIII was the most famous owner of Leeds Castle. He liked Leeds very much, often visited and spent huge sums enlarging and improving the building. He in effect turned Leeds Castle from a fortress into a palace. The Maidens' Tower was built for the visit of Henry VIII's first queen, to house her maids of honour. Among those maids was Anne Boleyn, from nearby Hever Castle.

Henry VIII gave Leeds to Sir Anthony St Leger, and the castle passed out of royal ownership. Eventually, in 1929, the castle was bought by Lady Olive Baillie. She completely restored the building again and lived in it longer than any other owner; once again Leeds became a lady's castle. In the Second World War, Lady Baillie offered the castle as a military hospital, and it became a convalescent home for airmen with severe burns. She finally left Leeds to the nation.

Leeds Castle, the Ladies' Castle, flies the flags of two ladies alternately – Eleanor of Castile, the first lady owner, and Lady Baillie, the last.

WALMER CASTLE

LOCATION **KENT, ENGLAND**

DATE BUILT **1538**

FOUNDER **KING HENRY VIII**

Walmer Castle belongs to the refortification programme set in motion by Henry VIII. There was a major invasion scare in 1538, when Henry's two Catholic enemies, the Holy Roman Emperor and the French king became reconciled.

Suddenly England was faced with the prospect of an imminent joint Imperial-French invasion. Lambarde, the Elizabethan historian of Kent, wrote that Henry VIII, 'determined to stand upon his own guard and defence; and without sparing any cost he built castles, platforms and blockhouses in all needful places of the Realm.'

Within just two years, Henry had accomplished an amazing feat; he had built the first comprehensive new defence system of southern Britain since Roman times. The Thames was fitted with five new forts. Next came three new castles intended to protect the anchorage in the Downs – Sandown, Deal and Walmer. Next came the set of four new castles to defend the Solent and finally the new castle at Portland. The overall scheme protected the English coast from the Thames estuary to Dorset, and it was almost entirely in place by 1540 – a remarkable achievement.

The design of these new-generation castles was very distinct, with an emphasis on huge round low bastions, yet there were elements that were inherited from the Norman castles too. Each had a central round tower, corresponding to the Norman keep; that central tower stood in a bailey with a bastioned curtain wall; it also had a moat. At Walmer, the circular curtain wall was only a little larger than the central tower, and it was dominated by its four huge bastions. It is not known how many guns Walmer carried in Henry's day, but by 1597 it was equipped with one cannon, one culverin, five demi-culverins, a saker, a minion and a falcon. The Walmer guns were effectively covering the Downs anchorage, as intended.

There were eleven trained gunners stationed at Walmer in Elizabeth I's post-Armada time, but presumably the manning was stepped up in times of national emergency. In the time of Charles II, the numbers were much the same.

Walmer Castle became the residence of the Warden of the Cinque Ports. The Duke of Wellington loved Walmer. He called it 'the most charming marine residence I have ever seen'. In old age, he spent as much time there as he could and died there.

HEVER CASTLE

LOCATION **KENT, ENGLAND**
DATE BUILT **1340/1384**
FOUNDER **SIR JOHN DE COBHAM**

Henry II deliberately accelerated the arms race, making state-of-the-art castle-building so expensive that only the elite could afford to stay in the race. The poorer barons had to be content with fortified manor houses. One outstanding example of those that have survived is Hever Castle.

Hever's first licence to crenellate is dated 1340, but the creation of the moat and the main defences came after a second licence was granted, in 1384, to Sir John de Cobham. The main motive for investing money in defence at that time was almost certainly the threat of a French invasion. The defensive works were maintained right through the 15th century, and it is likely that the occupants of Hever were fearful of predatory neighbours in Kent itself.

In 1462, Hever Castle was acquired by Sir Geoffrey Boleyn, a successful hatter who became Lord Mayor of London. It was famously the scene of Henry VIII's courtship of one of the daughters of the house, Anne Boleyn, a bitter-sweet historical association that still hangs heavy on the air at Hever Castle.

The most impressive feature is the colossal three-storeyed gatehouse, which seems far too big for this modest little castle. It is a high medieval take on the Norman keep, with drawbridge, portcullis, elaborate – and probably decorative – machicolation and battlements. There is also some decorative carved stonework above the gate and a pleasantly asymmetrical arrangement of windows, large and small. It is a very pretty building, but it would be vain to suppose that it would ever have withstood cannon-fire.

The Astor family took ownership of the castle, and undertook its restoration and modernization, turning it into a very comfortable home. The restoration work began in 1903 and cost a great deal of money. Part of the work involved landscaping the grounds. This included the creation of an artificial lake; a team of local labourers was hired to dig out the lake. Looking at the lake now, the labourers long gone, it is hard to believe that any human hand was involved in its creation.

DOVER CASTLE

LOCATION **KENT, ENGLAND**

DATE BUILT **1160s–1180s**

FOUNDER **KING HENRY II**

Although some keeps in the 1180s were being built in the new, experimental cylindrical shape, Dover Castle was given an old-fashioned square keep, even though it would have blind and vulnerable corners.

Dover's keep was a big cube, surrounded by a long curtain wall with 14 square towers and two powerful gatehouses. It cost £6,000. The keep was fitted with an ingenious plumbing system, but the overall architectural design showed no advance on the square keeps built 50 years earlier.

Dover, like other castles, took a long time to build. A keep 18.3 metres (60 ft) high would probably have taken six years to build. It was important to get the design right because of the cost in time, manpower and money, so it is strange that Dover was built to a design that would be obsolete when finished. It may be that Henry II was confident that the square keep would be secure within the outer defence system, which did incorporate innovations; it had immensely strong wall-towers and gatehouses. The projecting wall-towers effectively prevented the walls from being mined, because they could provide fire cover for every inch of the wall. With a really strong curtain wall, the strength of the keep became less important. The square designs were much easier to build and from a domestic point of view easier to live in.

The Angevin kings spent a huge amount of money on castles, and evidently believed their thrones depended on them. Between 1155 and 1215, they spent £46,000 on building castles. Henry II spent £21,000 on his castles, of which Dover was one. Henry III spent £85,000 in all on castles, about one-tenth of his annual income. He allocated £7,500 to updating Dover Castle. These outlays may look extravagant, but the monarchs recognized the need to defend themselves against untrustworthy barons. Henry II was also keen to force lesser barons out of the arms race; the fewer castle-owning barons there were, the more easily he could deal with them.

One significant innovation Henry's engineers introduced at Dover was a new kind of wall aperture – arrow-slits for crossbows in the Avranches Tower.

BODIAM CASTLE

LOCATION **EAST SUSSEX, ENGLAND**

DATE BUILT **1385**

FOUNDER **SIR EDWARD DALYNGRIGGE**

Bodiam is beautifully, almost classically, symmetrical, which satisfies the eye. It is set in the middle of a moat that's so wide the castle seems like a ship moored in a lake.

That view of the castle across the moat is the best thing about Bodiam. To venture across the causeway and inspect the interior is an anticlimax. The castle is a perfect but hollow shell, as empty as if it had been bombed.

It was in October 1385 that Sir Edward Dalyngrigge was granted a licence by Richard II to fortify his manor house. Both Rye and Winchelsea, ports not far from Bodiam, had been ravaged by the French in the previous few years. The king was pleased, in his own words, to let Dalyngrigge 'strengthen with a wall of stone and lime, and crenellate and make into a castle his manor house of Bodyham, near the sea, in the county of Sussex, for the defence of the adjacent county, and the resistance to our enemies'.

Dalyngrigge did not abide by the letter of the licence. He pulled down his manor house and built a full-scale stronghold instead, though in the event, the castle was never needed as a fortress. Sir Edward built modern conveniences into his castle – more than 30 wall fireplaces, a new invention – and it remained a dwelling through the 15th and 16th centuries.

The square castle has a fine round tower at each corner and a square tower projecting from the centre of each wall. The one on the north wall is developed into an elaborate gatehouse, with machicolated towers and a spiked portcullis. One range of buildings was reserved for the mercenary soldiers, regularly employed by the lord of the castle to defend it.

The moat, now only picturesque, was there to defend Bodiam, to supply it with fish, and to dispose of sewage; it would have been much less attractive then than now. Another drawback was the 300 pairs of pigeons roosting in a tower, which would have consumed a good proportion of the villagers' crops.

This is a castle without a history, the only incident a threat of a siege in the Wars of the Roses, but the Lewknor family surrendered. Yet Bodiam remains the quintessence of the middle ages and everyone's perfect castle.

HASTINGS CASTLE

LOCATION **EAST SUSSEX, ENGLAND**

DATE BUILT **1066**

FOUNDER **WILLIAM THE CONQUEROR**

After landing in Sussex in 1066, Duke William of Normandy raised two castles on the south coast in rapid succession: one of these was Hastings. It was a matter of urgency to secure his bridgehead in England and defend his position.

After strengthening the Roman fort of Pevensey, William had a castle built on the cliffs at Hastings, to protect his army from the east. While these building works were going on, King Harold's Saxon army was marching south. Hastings Castle was completed shortly before the great and decisive battle.

These two castles were built fast, out of timber, and William brought them with him in prefabricated kit form, in his ships. By 1070, the new king had issued orders that the castle of Hastings should be rebuilt in stone. It was the Count of Eu who held the castle at Hastings through the Norman period.

At one point, King John gave orders for Hastings Castle to be slighted to stop it falling into the hands of the French. In around 1220, Henry III ordered the refortification of the castle and it then flourished for 60 years.

In 1287, disaster struck. There were many months of severe weather. Storms ravaged the coastline and huge waves undermined the sandstone cliffs. Large sheets of rock collapsed into the sea, taking sections of the castle with them. There was also deforestation and more extensive ploughing in the Weald. This released tonnes of silt into the rivers, silting up harbours. Many south coast ports, including Hastings, suffered a decline. The castle was abandoned and the town impoverished.

In 1339 and 1377, when England was at war with France, Hastings was attacked by the French and badly damaged. Through the next hundred years, coastal erosion meant that even more of the castle was lost to the sea.

After the Dissolution the land was bought by the local Pelham family and used for farming. The remains of the neglected castle and church were rediscovered and excavated in 1824. The surviving walling was repaired and the place became a popular attraction for Victorian visitors. In the Second World War stray bombs added further damage to the almost total ruin.

BATTLE ABBEY

LOCATION **EAST SUSSEX, ENGLAND**

DATE BUILT **1070 (CONSECRATED 1094)**

FOUNDER **WILLIAM THE CONQUEROR**

Battle Abbey was founded by William the Conqueror to celebrate his famous conquest of England at the Battle of Hastings on 14 October 1066.

The abbey was built on the site of the battle itself, with the high altar deliberately placed on the spot where King Harold, the last Saxon king, raised his standard as the battle commenced.

The abbey housed Benedictine monks from Marmoutier, near Tours, and was consecrated in 1094. After the Dissolution in 1538, it was granted to Sir Anthony Brown, Master of the King's Horse. Brown set about destroying the church and adapting the monastic buildings for his own use.

The gatehouse, built in 1339, is an impressive structure with battlements and turrets, dominating the Market Square. Beyond the gatehouse are various buildings, some still inhabited, such as the abbot's lodge and two towers. Today the abbey is a girls' school.

The abbey church has almost completely vanished, except for part of the undercroft (crypt) of the church's eastern extension, which was erected in the 14th century and had five chapels. The foundations are marked out, though, and it is possible to gain from them an impression of the building's size. The chapterhouse lay to the south of the church's south transept.

Battle Abbey's most impressive remains are the monks' dormitory or dorter. Its undercroft is intact, with its three fine Early English chambers. The lower floor of this building marked the east side of the cloister, while the south wall of the church's nave made the cloister's north wall. The remains of a parlour can also be seen between the dorter and the chapter house. On the south side of the cloister is the frater, while the substantial kitchen can be seen on the far side.

Beyond this complex of buildings there is a fine walk with a splendid view across the valley where the fateful battle took place, still a patchwork of meadows and woods. From there it is possible to follow a route round the battlefield, and imagine the various stages in the Battle of Hastings.

PEVENSEY CASTLE

LOCATION **EAST SUSSEX, ENGLAND**

DATE BUILT **3RD AND 11TH CENTURIES**

FOUNDER **ROMANS AND WILLIAM THE CONQUEROR**

Pevensey is a really remarkable place – two very different castles for the price of one, and sitting one within the other. On the broad flat land of Pevensey Levels a slim peninsula projected into a large shallow bay. Here the Romans built one of their most impressive forts.

The fort was called Anderida. It was built in the third century AD to defend the so-called Saxon shore, the coastline of England most at threat from Saxon colonization. The Roman builders went to some trouble to make secure foundations for this fortress in the marsh, creating a bed of clay and flints. On top of this they placed oak beams set in concrete. Then, on top of that, they raised the massive curtain wall, 3.7 metres (12 ft) thick and almost 9.1 metres (30 ft) high. It was made of mortared flint rubble faced with stone.

This Roman curtain wall was an immense structure, punctuated with squat round towers or bastions, and it enclosed a huge area of more than 3.2 hectares (8 acres). Most incredibly of all, this magnificent fortress still stands intact after 1,600 years, even though it has seen repeated military action and has been besieged several times over.

The first attack on Anderida that we know about is recorded in the Anglo-Saxon Chronicle. In the fifth century, Aelle, the first Saxon King of Sussex, and his son Cissa laid siege to Andredeceaster (the fort of Anderida), 'and slew all the inhabitants; there was not even one Briton left there'. Evidently the local Britons had taken refuge in the old Roman fort, but Aelle ruthlessly massacred them regardless. This merciless and decisive rout firmly established Aelle as the unchallenged King of Sussex and he emerged as the first 'bretwalda', or commander-in-chief, of the Anglo-Saxons.

The walls of the Roman fortress were still complete when Duke William of Normandy sailed his invasion fleet into Pevensey Bay 600 years later. The Conqueror occupied the magnificent old fort and immediately erected his very first English timber castle inside it. It is said that he brought this first timber castle across in kit form in his ships. The fine old Roman walls of Anderida

made a perfect outer bailey, and indeed may even have suggested a blueprint for later English castles built from scratch that were to follow.

In time, the initial early Norman timber castle was replaced by a stone castle. This happened after Robert of Mortain, William's half-brother, had been granted Pevensey. The inner defences gradually took shape round the Norman keep during the 13th century; these consisted of a moat, a wall and a gatehouse with two towers. The new curtain wall of the inner bailey was built in architectural imitation of the Roman curtain wall by having three D-shaped towers, just like the Roman bastions.

Pevensey both triumphed and failed defensively. For example, William Rufus starved Pevensey into surrender, but King Stephen and Simon de Montfort both laid siege to Pevensey and failed to make it yield. At the close of the 14th century, Pevensey was once again successfully defended, this time by Lady Jane Pelham against the allies of the deposed Richard II; her husband was away fighting in the north of England. Lady Jane wrote to her husband, 'And my dear Lord, if it like you to know my fare, I am here laid by in manner of a siege … so that I may not out nor no victuals get me, but with much hard.'

By 1400, Pevensey Castle was no longer standing in a bay but in a saltmarsh. The shingle spit known as the Crumbles was building gradually across the entrance to the bay and turning it into an increasingly sheltered expanse of marsh. Pevensey, like some other south coast ports – Steyning, Rye and Winchelsea – was being left behind by the sea, thanks to accelerating silting. As a result, Pevensey was gradually losing its importance as a coastal fortress.

It was, even so, fortified against the Spanish Armada in 1588. A gun called a demi-culverin, and made of local Wealden iron, still stands within the castle's inner bailey. Even during the Second World War the location was seen as having a strategic significance, and gun emplacements were built to defend this stretch of coastline against a landing of German tanks and infantry. But the fabric of the castle itself had long since fallen into rack and ruin. In the 17th century, when the Parliamentary commissioners surveyed it, Pevensey Castle was already in a state of neglect. Curiously, the Roman walls are now in a better state than the Norman walls, even though they are a thousand years older.

Many medieval castles were made very comfortable, but Pevensey seems to have remained fairly austere. Domestic considerations had to give way to the requirements of military strength. Here it was that the young Thomas Becket was sent as a boy by his father, to learn the ways of gentlemen; it was customary in the middle ages to send upper class boys away to be schooled in a castle belonging to a stranger. Pevensey must have been a particularly hard school for the young Becket.

Pevensey Castle is a wonderfully tangible link with several epoch-making episodes in English history; with the Roman conquest, with the threat and the actuality of the Saxon invasion, with the emergence of a pan-Saxon war-leader, with the Norman invasion and the consolidation of that conquest, with the boyhood of England's greatest medieval saint, with the threatened Spanish and German invasions, and above all with the shifting shape of the coastline of England.

HERSTMONCEUX CASTLE

LOCATION **EAST SUSSEX, ENGLAND**

DATE BUILT **1441**

FOUNDER **SIR ROGER FIENNES**

Herstmonceux Castle is unusual in being a fairly late creation as far as castle-building goes. Sir Roger Fiennes was granted a licence for his fortified structure in 1441.

Herstmonceux is also unusual in being built of Flemish brick, and it was one of the first great buildings to be brick-built. Brick is, of course, more suited to house-building than castle-building.

Herstmonceux was built in a lake, so that the water could function as a moat. The water also had the effect of providing a reflection of the castle and making it appear loftier than it was. The aptly named Fiennes was Treasurer to the Household of Henry VI, and he was rich enough and of high enough status to build himself a truly splendid house.

The most striking feature of the castle is the gatehouse with its two imposing two-tiered towers rising 26 metres (84 ft) on either side of the entrance arch and drawbridge. The appearance is all too telling; these brick walls would never have withstood a cannon ball, let alone an artillery bombardment. Luckily they were never put to the test. The large square castle with its many towers and chimneys is nevertheless a very impressive sight. Its interior was well-appointed, and designed more for comfort than defence.

Some of the castle's later owners did not invest enough in maintenance. By the close of the 18th century, the Revd Robert Hare had used it as building materials for his new house, Herstmonceux Place. This reduced it to a ruin.

In the early 20th century, the castle was resurrected by Sir Claude Lowther. By referring back to the original plans, the ruins were transformed into an impressive home and the fine red brick exterior of the castle was faithfully restored to its original state.

In 1946, Herstmonceux became the home of the Royal Greenwich Observatory, to exploit the cleaner air of the countryside and the lack of light pollution. The Observatory remained at Herstmonceux until 1989.

LEWES CASTLE

LOCATION EAST SUSSEX, ENGLAND

DATE BUILT *c.* 1070

FOUNDER WILLIAM DE WARENNE

As a follower of Duke William of Normandy, William de Warenne was rewarded for his support of the Conqueror with lands in Sussex, Surrey and Norfolk. He built castles at Reigate and Castle Acre, but his main focus was Lewes.

At Lewes he built the castle that would be his family's residence for almost 300 years. De Warenne decided to visit Rome with his wife Gundrada, but they stopped in Burgundy, where they visited the Abbey of Cluny. As a result of this visit, on his return de Warenne founded a Cluniac priory at Lewes.

Lewes was an important Saxon township before the Normans arrived. Possibly a Saxon castle formerly stood on the site of de Warenne's castle.

Lewes Castle is unusual in having two chalk mottes or castle mounds, one at each end of a level oval bailey. Late in the 11th century an oval shell-keep was raised on the south-western mound. A rectangular gatehouse was built to make an entrance on the south and the court or bailey was surrounded with a flint-faced wall. Surviving wall fragments show courses of large flints laid in a herringbone pattern, typical of early Norman masonry.

The keep has been partially destroyed. The walls on the north and east sides have gone. There have also been modifications to turn it into a kind of folly. The porch and circular stair to the south tower are all 19th century. The very attractive projecting towers were added much earlier, in the 13th century.

The southern tower is quite well preserved, though a second storey has been inserted. The roof and parapets are modern. In spite of all this modern interference, it is still worth going up the tower for the sake of the splendid view of the town of Lewes and the Brookland beyond.

The fine barbican or outer gatehouse built in the 14th century is by far the best feature of Lewes Castle. Barbicans were frequently left unroofed, but the Lewes barbican has a roof. It stands three storeys tall, with two round towers defending the southern entrance. They are linked at the top by a line of machicolations. The flintwork is very high quality, of squared knapped flint, and a fine early example of this kind of masonry.

ARUNDEL CASTLE

LOCATION **WEST SUSSEX, ENGLAND**

DATE BUILT **1067**

FOUNDER **ROGER DE MONTGOMERY**

After the Conquest, William gave the earldom of Arundel to Roger de Montgomery, who contributed 60 ships to the invasion fleet. He also ordered Roger to build a castle on the Arun to protect the valley route to the interior.

The origins of Arundel are obscure. What we see today is a heavily reconstructed 18th and 19th century baronial version of the ancient castle. Whatever was there before, Roger started building his motte and bailey timber fort at Arundel in 1067. He designed it with a motte between two baileys instead of the usual single bailey. The earthworks are still in good condition. The original wooden fort was gradually replaced in stone.

When Montgomery's son, Robert, rebelled against Henry I in 1102, Arundel Castle and his lands were taken from him. After Henry I's death, Arundel passed to his second wife Adelaide of Louvain; in 1138 she married William d'Albini and they made their home at Arundel Castle. William built an outstanding shell-keep using Caen stone and Quarr Abbey stone.

When d'Albini died, the castle passed to Henry II, who stayed there in 1182 and on other occasions, spending huge sums on improvements. Under Richard I, Arundel was passed back to the d'Albini family. Then the Fitzalan family took it. In 1555, it passed into the Howard family, where it remains.

In 1787, the 11th Duke, Charles Howard, who was a keen architect, decided to reconstruct Arundel Castle to his own design. The works were completed in 1815 at a cost of £600,000. Henry Granville, the 14th duke, started yet another reconstruction, but died before it was finished. The work was finished in 1900, with many internal features of the earlier reconstructions retained. The overall effect is grand and imposing, but the castle looks best when glimpsed from a distance, rising romantically out of the downland beech hangers.

The 15th duke added many modern touches: electric lights, fire-fighting equipment, service lifts, central heating. For a long time, the ancient keep was left unrestored, as a picturesque ruin inhabited by a colony of owls.

COWDRAY HOUSE

LOCATION **WEST SUSSEX, ENGLAND**

DATE BUILT **1492**

FOUNDER **SIR DAVID OWEN**

It was on 24 September 1793 that a workman at Cowdray House, a splendid Tudor mansion at the foot of the South Downs near Midhurst, absent-mindedly left a fire unattended. By the end of that day one of the finest houses in Sussex had gone up in smoke.

Founded in 1492 by Sir David Owen, son of Owen Glendower, Cowdray House had, at the time of the fire, been standing for more than 300 years. Like many mansions, Cowdray was modified over the decades by successive owners. Sir William Fitzwilliam made changes after buying the house and estate in 1529. When he died in 1542, the still uncompleted house passed into the hands of his half-brother Sir Anthony Brown, who owned Bayham and Battle Abbeys. Brown was Henry VIII's Master of Horse. When Sir Anthony died in 1548, Cowdray House was complete.

The great park, later landscaped by Capability Brown, was a suitable setting for entertaining royalty. Edward VI was entertained at Cowdray – in fact the young king said that he had been 'rather excessively banqueted there'. Sir Anthony's son, who became the first Lord Montague, entertained Elizabeth I, who never complained that hospitality was too lavish. She shot some of Montague's deer in the park.

But the magnificence of Cowdray all came to an end in 1793. The ruins stand, frozen in their 1793 state, showing still the beautiful Tudor stonework in an impressively consistent, fine, sober, English Renaissance style. Refreshingly, the ruins of Cowdray have not been 'smartened up' in the way that many other historic buildings in England have.

There is a turreted gatehouse, a great hall with huge bay windows and stone transoms and mullions, and many domestic buildings as well, all ranged round a square courtyard. The hall originally had a fine hammerbeam roof of oak timbers; it was known as the Buck Hall because of the life-sized bucks portrayed on the walls bearing heraldic shields. The Cowdray chapel had a three-sided apse with a large window in each wall and a battlemented roof.

CARISBROOKE CASTLE

LOCATION ISLE OF WIGHT, ENGLAND
DATE BUILT PRE-ROMAN FORT, 1136 (FIRST STONE STRUCTURE)
FOUNDER BALDWIN DE REDVERS (NORMAN CASTLE)

Carisbrooke has some unusual associations; Charles I sat in its window seats, stammering politely to his captors as he looked out across the village, futilely planning his escape.

Carisbrooke is one of the most ancient fortresses in England. A fort probably stood here before the Romans arrived, and when they came they raised a stronghold with a rectangular curtain wall. The Saxons occupied the site after a fierce and bloody battle, and it was probably the Saxons who raised the huge artificial mound which was later to carry the Norman shell-keep.

The first stone structure on the site appears to have been raised in 1136, when Baldwin de Redvers held the Isle of Wight. The shell-keep was built then, and so was the curtain wall surrounding the west bailey. During the middle ages, Carisbrooke withstood several attacks from the French. The Norman defences remained intact, but the domestic buildings were repeatedly rebuilt. The great hall and ancillary buildings were in place by 1299.

The gatehouse, which is the most impressive feature, was built in 1335, though the beautiful parapets and machicolations were added in about 1470. The entrance arch between two stout round towers consists of several arches recessed one within another, creating an effect of enormous solidity. The gatehouse is defended by three portcullises and a moat with a stone bridge.

In the Elizabethan period, the threat from Spain justified extensive improvements. The domestic ranges were brought up to date and some outer defences were added. It was probably at this time that Carisbrooke Castle's famous well – 60 metres (200 ft) deep – was dug.

The castle was in this upgraded state when Charles I arrived in 1647, optimistically expecting to find sanctuary as well as sympathy from Colonel Hammond, the governor. Hammond, however, owed his appointment to Cromwell, so although he treated Charles graciously, soon the king became a prisoner. Charles's attempted escape was a fiasco.

Carisbrooke Castle was the island governor's residence until 1944. After that the main house was converted into an Isle of Wight Museum.

BATH ABBEY

LOCATION **BATH & NORTH EAST SOMERSET, ENGLAND**

DATE BUILT **1499**

FOUNDER **BISHOP OLIVER KING**

Bath Abbey, dedicated to St Peter and St Paul, was the last of the great pre-Reformation churches to be built. The abbey stands in the centre of the town, close to the Roman Baths.

The abbey has a conventional cross-shaped plan, with a tower at the crossing. The tower is unusual, in being rectangular rather than square because of the narrow transepts and wide nave and choir. The most outstanding feature is its west front, which has a magnificent window. On each side are turrets with ladders to heaven carved on them, with angels passing up and down.

The site has a long and remarkable history, beginning as an Iron Age religious site, with hot springs as the focus of a pagan sanctuary dedicated to a goddess called Sul. During the Roman occupation, this was developed by the Romans, who called the place Aquae Sulis. The Saxons took it over in 577 and renamed it Hat Bathu ('At the Baths'). In 676, a Christian king called Osric endowed a religious house which was both a monastery and a nunnery.

By the tenth century, Bath had become such an important focus that Edgar was crowned King of England there in 973. A hundred years later, under Norman rule, work was begun on a cathedral, on the site of the present abbey. Very little of the Norman church, built by Bishop John de Villula, has survived other than a single arch in the south-east corner of the abbey church.

De Villula transferred the seat of his bishopric from Wells to Bath, and in the 13th century the Pope confirmed the title 'Bishop of Bath and Wells'. Though Wells is now the only bishopric in Somerset the title remains.

After 1122 Bath Abbey entered a period of decline. In 1499 Bishop Oliver King began work on a completely new church, on the same site, but much smaller than the old one. The entire length of the present building fits onto the site of the Norman nave, making it about half the length of its predecessor. Bishop King had a vision of angels, which inspired him to build the church, and which is commemorated in the carvings on the west front.

The Dissolution delayed completion and it was not consecrated until 1616. The interior was restored by Sir Gilbert Scott in the 1860s.

NUNNEY CASTLE

LOCATION **SOMERSET, ENGLAND**

DATE BUILT **1373**

FOUNDER **SIR JOHN DE LA MARE**

Nunney Castle sits placidly in the middle of Nunney village, south-west of Frome, and is as far from being an oppressive and forbidding seat of military power as could be imagined.

Nunney was in fact never intended to be a real fortress, but a high-status mansion, and must have been a picturesque folly even when it was built. The big, drum-shaped angle-towers give an impression of solidity and strength, but close examination reveals that they are built of rather small stones, not the sort of masonry to withstand a cannon ball or a battering ram.

Nunney is a four-storey tower-house, and it was built in 1373 by Sir John de la Mare (or Delamere), using the proceeds of his fighting in the Hundred Years War. The rectangular keep has cylindrical towers at its corners and the building as a whole is surrounded by a moat. The central feature is a courtyard, but the corner towers are built so close together that the courtyard was virtually squeezed out, leaving just a light well. This was the practice at some French castles, and it looks as if Sir John brought back the idea for Nunney's design from his French campaigning, along with the money to pay for it. It is a French-influenced example of a 'collapsed courtyard' castle.

This arrangement was originally set in a bailey surrounded by a curtain wall on three sides and a stream on the fourth, but these defences would not have kept Nunney safe from even a casual attack.

Sir John was really dressing up his luxury home a little and wanted the status of being a castle-dwelling war veteran, but he was evidently not expecting any serious trouble. Nor was there any. The de la Mares handed their castle on intact to the Paulets and the Praters. A small but dangerous resistance was made on the king's behalf in the Civil War, though, and for that it was slighted by Cromwell's men. The north side of the castle was so weakened by this slighting that as recently as 1910 it fell down to expose the interior, where chambers, garderobes and spiral stairs can be seen.

In Nunney Castle, we can share an elderly medieval knight's nostalgia for military glory, and dream the old campaigner's dream of knightly chivalry.

GLASTONBURY ABBEY

LOCATION **SOMERSET, ENGLAND**

DATE BUILT **1213 (ON SITE OF EARLIER ABBEY)**

FOUNDER **MONASTIC COMMUNITY**

Glastonbury Abbey is still a noble and inspiring sight, though it is only a fragment of what originally stood on this unusual spot, a hill rising sharply out of the Somerset Levels.

When the abbey was dissolved in 1539, it was unroofed and the walls left open to the weather. The shell of the great abbey then served as a quarry for building stone; much of the town of Glastonbury was built out of blocks scavenged from the huge church and its ancillary buildings.

None of the visible walls is older than 1184. There was an abbey on the site before, but after a devastating fire in 1184 a total rebuild was needed. Only one chamber and the bell tower were left of the magnificent monastery with its abbey church that had been the resting place of many saints.

The story of that older abbey was long and distinguished, and it was assembled by one of the leading medieval historians, William of Malmesbury. At the invitation of the Glastonbury monks, William wrote a book on Glastonbury's history. Unfortunately, he was a guest at the abbey and felt an obligation to please his hosts, so the story was inflated with some incredible legends. He begins the story with King Lucius, a legendary British ruler who is supposed to have lived in the second century. Lucius travelled to Rome, where Pope Eleutherius supplied him with missionaries. Lucius returned, converted the people and founded the Church of St Mary at Glastonbury. This story had for a long time been 'authorized' by Bede, but William also quoted another legend, in which the monks audaciously attributed the founding of Glastonbury to the disciples of Christ. William evidently did not believe this, writing that he would 'leave disputable matters'.

The site of Glastonbury is a hilly peninsula, a finger of land pointing out into the marshes. On the neck of the peninsula is a massive earthwork, Ponter's Ball, raised in the late Iron Age. This suggests that Glastonbury was an important pagan sanctuary. Holy precincts at that time were often associated with hills beside springs and Glastonbury shares this association. The main spring on the island, Chalice Well, lies immediately below the

summit, Glastonbury Tor. The existence of a great pagan sanctuary on the Isle of Glastonbury would explain the interest shown in the site by Christians. Pope Gregory instructed that Christian missionaries should take over pagan sanctuaries and then win the pagans round gradually to Christian rites.

The core and centre of the new Christian monastery was the ancient cemetery round the Lady Chapel, which was built on the site of the older Church of St Mary. Within and beside this cemetery were small oratories built of wattle and daub. It was in this ancient cemetery that the monks perpetrated their most shameless fraud; they claimed that they found the bodies of King Arthur and his queen there.

The great church, as it was later described, was begun late in the 12th century and enough of it was finished for the monks to take possession at Christmas 1213. It consisted of a choir of seven bays for the monks, with two side aisles, a very long nave of nine bays, also with two side aisles, two massive transepts and a spacious crossing under a soaring central tower. At the eastern end of this colossus there was an additional chapel, called the Edgar Chapel, which was built on later. At the western end there was the final addition, a spacious porch called the Galilee, built in the 14th century, which linked the new church building with the old Lady Chapel, making it an amazing 161 metres (530 ft) long overall.

The great church was one of the finest religious buildings ever to be built in England. The loss of this architectural masterpiece is one of the scandals of Henry VIII's reign. To the south of this endless church was a large cloister, a chapter house, a refectory, a kitchen and a dormitory. Separate, and to the south-west, were the abbot's hall and kitchen. To the north of that lay the site of the ancient cemetery, now levelled up to make a pleasant garden.

The great church needed to be a splendid and spectacular building to attract pilgrims, who were

the basis of the tourist industry of the middle ages. Here we have the motive for the monks' fabrication of the Arthur and Guinevere graves. The legends gave the Glastonbury experience a special edge over other pilgrimage centres. The great church itself was a spectacular focus that pulled the pilgrims (and their money) in from all over England and mainland Europe. Like Canterbury and Santiago de Compostela, Glastonbury was one of the major pilgrimage centres of Europe.

The enormous wealth of Glastonbury caught Henry VIII's eye. His commissioners reported that 'the house is greate, goodly, and so pryncely as we have not sene the lyke'. The abbot, who lived like a duke, was a man of 80 and not about to change his ways. Richard Whiting refused to surrender his abbey. Worse, he hid the abbey's plate to stop the king getting hold of it. The elderly abbot was arrested, charged with treason and tried, though the trial was a sham. On 15 November 1539, the white-haired abbot was dragged on a hurdle to the summit of Glastonbury Tor, where he was hanged, drawn and quartered. It was by any standards a terrible thing Cromwell had done in Henry VIII's name. And then the abbey itself underwent its martyrdom, its stones torn out for shops and houses and to pave the road to Wells.

OLD WARDOUR CASTLE

LOCATION **WILTSHIRE, ENGLAND**

DATE BUILT **1393**

FOUNDER **SIR JOHN LOVELL**

Old Wardour Castle, between Shaftesbury and Wilton, lies buried in the depths of rural Wiltshire. Built in the late 14th century, its design was influenced by the French style.

The castle, or rather keep, stands in the middle of a bailey surrounded by a curtain wall, but it is clear that this was a mansion rather than a fortress. The original fortified house was raised in 1393, when Sir John Lovell was granted a licence to crenellate. It was built round a small six-sided courtyard, with large square towers at the corners. Lovell was a veteran of the French wars and he modelled his castle on a French courtyard castle.

Old Wardour Castle was modernized in the 16th century after Sir Matthew Arundell bought the castle. Most of the architectural details on the house belong to that 'restoration' phase. The Arundells were Royalists, so in 1646 the 25 defenders of Old Wardour Castle found themselves besieged by a thousand Parliamentarian soldiers. The defence was led by Lady Blanche Arundell. The Parliamentarian troops began undermining the walls, so Lady Blanche surrendered. After the women and children had been led away into captivity, the soldiers wantonly damaged the house and grounds.

The following year, the Royalists' laid siege to Old Wardour, but the Parliamentarians resisted for longer than was expected, thanks to the inspiring leadership of Robert Balsom. The Royalists had meanwhile done a lot of damage to the house and the castle was mined – by Lord Arundell himself – to make sure no one else got his castle.

The Arundell family built a new mansion nearby, but did not demolish the old one. The ruin stands as a monument to the madness of war. Lady Blanche did everything she could to defend her family's castle, yet she later had to watch as her husband blew the castle up as a point of principle.

The grounds of the ruins were landscaped in romantic style, and the elaborate Tudor alterations are still visible.

CORFE CASTLE

LOCATION **DORSET, ENGLAND**

DATE BUILT **11TH CENTURY (REBUILDING OF EARLIER STRUCTURE)**

FOUNDER **WILLIAM THE CONQUEROR**

Corfe Castle is a dramatic ruin in a dramatic setting, standing on a steep-sided, natural conical hill commanding the narrow, ravine-like gap through the chalk ridge that defends the Isle of Purbeck.

This gap was once called 'Corvesgate'. On each side, to north and south, are expanses of desolate heathland. The castle stands in the narrow gap like a soldier in a sentry box – very much on guard duty.

There was a castle here at least as early as the tenth century, well before the Norman conquest. It was rebuilt by the Normans, modernized and completed in the 13th century after being re-created in stone in the reigns of King John and Edward I. Then, and for four centuries after, Corfe Castle must have been one of the most imposing fortresses in England. It was totally impregnable until weapon technology enabled fire power to reach it from the hills to east and west.

The Norman castle builders used the same local Purbeck limestone that was used to build the village that grew up beside the castle, a village of quarrymen and stone carvers. Through that busy village of quarrymen and master masons passed armed troops on their way to and from the castle, and also kings and queens and their retinues.

Corfe Castle was the scene of a historic assassination, the murder of the Saxon King Edward the Martyr. In 978, the castle probably consisted of no more than a few domestic buildings within an inner ward of stone, surrounded by a timber palisade. There was a gatehouse on the south side, giving access to the castle from the village. The boy-king was arriving at the gatehouse, when he was stabbed to death while being greeted by his step-mother. It was she who master-minded the murder. Fatally stabbed, the youth tried to ride away, but fainted and fell from his horse. His foot caught in the stirrup and he was dragged along by his horse. Miracles were claimed, and the dead king was subsequently proclaimed a saint and martyr.

The castle was rebuilt on William the Conqueror's orders, and in 1100 it was fitted with a large keep and a large outer bailey built of stone, giving it

The ruinous state of Corfe Castle is a direct result of slighting by the Parliamentarians in 1646.

something close to its appearance today. The keep was a bleak, austere, thick-walled cube 21 metres (70 ft) high. It was reached by a path that wound up the slope, passing through one defence after another. The already strong fortress was further strengthened by King John; he wanted to use it as a state prison and a strong-room for the crown jewels. The butavant or dungeon tower was raised at the western edge of the west bailey, where very steep slopes made a natural defence. Among King John's prisoners here were 22 French aristocrats. John ordered that they should be given neither food nor water. Their deaths added another crime to the list of dark

deeds committed at Corfe Castle. King John murdered his nephew Duke Arthur of Brittany with his own hands, then imprisoned Arthur's sister Eleanor at Corfe for many years before moving her on to Bristol, where she died after spending most of her life in pointless captivity.

John extended the curtain walls and strengthened the existing buildings at Corfe. He also built the gloriette range round a courtyard; this was evidently an important addition, though what its use was is not clear.

Henry III had the chapel built and ordered the whole castle to be whitewashed. It made good practical sense to whitewash the interior, because the windows were very small and it was the only way to make the chambers light. Sometimes the exteriors of castles were also painted white, perhaps to make them more conspicuous, perhaps to cover up variations in the quality of masonry and possible weak points.

Corfe later became a prison for another distinguished royal prisoner, the deposed Edward II, who was kept there for a while before being taken to Berkeley Castle, where it is generally believed he was murdered. The king's brother, the Earl of Kent, did not believe he had been murdered at all, but still languished in the dungeons at Corfe. The Constable of Corfe Castle encouraged him to think this. The earl sent messages to his (probably) dead brother via the constable, but the constable delivered them to Queen Isabella and Roger Mortimer; it was not long before they arranged for the earl to vanish too.

Eventually Elizabeth I inherited Corfe Castle, and she gave it to one her favourites, Sir Christopher Hatton. In the 17th century, it passed into the ownership of Sir John Bankes, the Attorney General. In 1643, when Sir John Bankes was away, the castle was surrounded by a Parliamentarian army and Lady Bankes had to defend it herself. This she did very successfully for three years. In the end it was a Royalist island in a huge region occupied by Parliamentarian troops. It was only taken when one of the defending officers, Colonel Pitman, betrayed Lady Bankes by letting the Parliamentary soldiers in.

Parliament immediately ordered the slighting of Corfe Castle. The foundations of the castle's defences were quarried away and the buildings were blown up with gunpowder. Some walls collapsed down the hillside. Some towers tilted out of the perpendicular. The south tower of the gatehouse, sometimes called Edward the Martyr's Gate, was broken away from its foundations and blown sideways, so that it now stands, upright and intact, some metres from its original position. This is one of the visitors' first sights of the castle, approaching the gatehouse from the picturesque village.

The slighting was so thorough and so effective that the castle was not only indefensible but uninhabitable. It was never again lived in after 1646.

Instead, Corfe Castle became – in the space of a few days – the archetypal ruined castle, the ultimate Gothic folly. Although it arrived at its ruinous state suddenly and all at once, it somehow epitomizes in people's minds the distance between the present day and England's historic past. As a result, it attracts many more visitors than castles that remain intact.

ST MICHAEL'S MOUNT

LOCATION **CORNWALL, ENGLAND**
DATE BUILT **1135**
FOUNDER **BERNARD LE BEC**

St Michael's Mount is a granite crag rising startlingly out of the sea in the middle of St Michael's Bay, accessible on foot only at low tide across a causeway. It is a superb site for a castle, but it has had a very mixed use.

This little rocky island's long history began during the Neolithic Age with the coastwise trade in stone axes, and it went on to become a major port in the Iron Age.

The Mount has also found its way into several strands of British legend, including the stories of Tristan and Isolde and Jack the Giant Killer. The giant Cormoran, who lived on it, used to wade ashore and snatch cows to eat. Jack is alleged to have killed Cormoran by blowing on his horn and getting the giant to run down the hillside into a pit. The pit or well, now sealed, is still visible.

Diodorus Siculus described how St Michael's Mount became a major trading post in the Iron Age. 'They convey [Cornish tin] to an island which lies off Britain and is called Ictis; for at the ebb-tide the space between this island and the mainland becomes dry and they can take the tin in large quantities over to the islands on their wagons. On the island of Ictis, the [Greek] merchants purchase the tin from the natives and carry it to Galatia or Gaul.'

The island's dedication dates from AD 495, when a group of fishermen standing on a ledge high on the island's western side had a vision of St Michael.

After the Norman Conquest, much of the West Country was given to Robert Count of Mortain, who

The tidal rocky island makes an impregnable
site for a fortress.

became Earl of Cornwall. Robert in turn granted the Mount
to the Norman Abbey of Mont St Michel; a priory was
established there in 1135 by Bernard of Le Bec. The site
nevertheless made it ideal for a fortress. In the 12th century
it was seized and held as a fortress by some of Prince John's
supporters while Richard I was away. Afterwards the rock
returned to its monastic use, but it was seized by Henry V
during the war with France, and by 1424 all links between
the Mount and its French counterpart were severed. The
Mount was once more used as a fortress in the Wars of the
Roses and the Cornish Rebellion against Edward VI.

The last time St Michael's Mount was used as a fortress
was in 1646, during the Civil War. It was held for a while
by Royalist supporters, but they were obliged to surrender
to Parliamentarian troops. The Mount was bought by the
last military governor of the Mount, Sir John St Aubyn,
in 1660 and since then has led an uninterrupted peaceful
existence. For many years the house was used by the St
Aubyns as a second home, mainly during the summer, but
during the 18th century they established it as their principal
home, adding a large new wing with impressive Victorian
apartments. The St Aubyn family owned St Michael's
Mount until 1964, when it was handed over to the
National Trust.

INDEX

PICTURE CREDITS

METRO BOOKS
New York

An Imprint of Sterling Publishing
387 Park Avenue South
New York, NY 10016

METRO BOOKS and the distinctive Metro Books logo are trademarks of Sterling Publishing Co., Inc.

© 2012 Quercus Editions Ltd

This 2012 edition published by Metro Books by arrangement with Quercus Publishing Plc

Designed and edited by
Topics – The Creative Partnership

ISBN 978-1-4351-3896-4

For information about custom editions, special sales, and premium and corporate purchases, please contact Sterling Special Sales at 800-805-5489 or specialsales@sterlingpublishing.com.

Manufactured in China

2 4 6 8 10 9 7 5 3

www.sterlingpublishing.com